DATE DUE

GAYLORD 234			PRINTED IN U. S. A.

MEN OF DESTINY

MEN OF DESTINY

by
PETER MASTERS

THE EVANGELICAL TIMES * LONDON

1968
THE EVANGELICAL TIMES LTD * LONDON
Distributed by
Hughes & Colman Ltd.,
Spar Road, Norwich

Set in Aldine Roman by The Evangelical Times
Printed by Fletcher & Son Ltd., Norwich
Bound by Richard Clay (The Chaucer Press) Ltd.
Bungay, Suffolk

CONTENTS

AUTHOR'S NOTE

While these biographies are short, the reader may be assured that they are the product of intensive research, extending in many cases to every single published work or available manuscript.

Special thanks are due to:-

Lady Beatrix Evison, for information and private papers of Viscount Alexander of Hillsborough; Mrs Sybil Johnston, for data and illustrations of General Sir William Dobbie; Mr. Peter Howell, who did the research for the life of Newton; Mr. David Rhodes and Mr. Andrew Pay for help on the lives of Fletcher and Luther.

Illustrations have been drawn from many sources, but special acknowledgements are due to Warner-Pathe Ltd. ('The Retreat from Moscow') The Welcome Trustees (Sir James Simpson) The Maritime Museum (John Newton) and the Union Castle Line (Captain Brown).

In conclusion, I join the numerous writers who acknowledge their dependence on the incredible facilities of the British Museum Library.

P.M.

FOREWORD

I welcome the publication of these articles, which have already appeared in the Evangelical Times, in this permanent form. I do so for many reasons. Throughout my Christian life I have found that, next to the Bible itself, nothing has given me greater help and encouragement than the reading of biographies of great Christians of various ages and countries.

Our danger is always to think that our problems are unique and our lot exceptionally hard. Thus we tend to become despondent and fearful. The finest antidote to that is to read the stories of great heroes of the faith of past ages. As we do so we are both shamed and also encouraged. That is what will happen to those who read this book.

At the same time it will serve what is a yet more important function, and especially at this present time. So many people today think one's attitude to Christianity is purely a psychological matter. If you belong to a certain type or group, or have a particular religious "complex", then you will be a Christian. They argue that it has nothing to do with objective truth but is purely a matter of our particular make-up.

Others fondly believe that it is purely a matter of intelligence and that no intelligent, educated, integrated person can possibly be a Christian. The simple answer to that is to be found, quite simply, in the history of the Christian church. Nothing is so amazing as the way in which people of every conceivable psychological type, and of all possible grades of intellect and knowledge, have been found worshipping God together as Christians.

That is the thing that is brought out so clearly and unmistakedly in the series of biographies found in this book. How different these men were on the surface, and by nature; but how united in their faith in the One Lord and Saviour Jesus Christ.

Here, then, at one and the same time, is a challenge to the sceptic and a comfort for the saint. I wish it a very wide and large circulation.

1968   **D. M. LLOYD-JONES**

THE TSAR WHO CRUSHED NAPOLEON

Czar Alexandre Pavlovich

For centuries, sovereigns, presidents and prime ministers have ruled by constitutions and cabinets. But Alexander Pavlovich, Tsar of Russia, was one of the great exceptions. By birth and by right, he was the 'Emperor of all Russia', dominating his massive land with the undisputed sway of a dictator.

He was Tsar of the rich nobility, with all its colourful splendour, and Tsar of the serfs, with their thousands of primitive hovels. He was the Tsar who liberated Europe by breaking the iron grip of Napoleon, ushering in his momentous fall and defeat. But powerful though he was, Alexander was a man who became inwardly overpowered and humbled in a way which was to dramatically change his whole way of life.

Alexander was the son of the Emperor Paul—a brutal Tsar who produced such chaos in Russia, that most people thought him insane. As Grand Duke and heir to the throne, Alexander saw very little of his notorious father, and was completely educated and trained by a Swiss tutor, who taught him to scorn Christ as "a Jew from whom the sect of Christians take their name". On one of the very few occasions when the future Tsar went into his father's presence, and knelt before his throne, the Emperor kicked him savagely in the face. This was the kind of treatment he gave everyone. Even countesses had been flogged at his command.

It was almost inevitable that by the time Alexander was twenty-four, a Palace revolution had been arranged to get rid of Paul and declare his son Tsar.

As Paul's cruelty increased, he grew more afraid for his safety and built a powerful fortress-palace in St. Petersburg, where he could rest behind fifteen-feet thick walls. But he could not protect himself from his own Palace staff. One night in 1801, sixty Palace officials rushed into his bedroom, murdered him, forced his physician to sign a false death certificate, and went out to proclaim Alexander as Tsar.

The son started his reign with thoughts of being the great reformer of the land. He dismissed all the old ministers of state and gathered round him a bunch of young intellectual friends who were called 'The Committee of Public Safety'. Daily, they held sessions to discuss the liberation of the serfs, and the countless other problems involved in bringing a backward nation to freedom and advancement. But they all lacked the dynamic and determination to DO anything, and after two years, their talk dried up and they miserably faded out. Alexander was disheartened and disillusioned. Although he was married to Princess Elizabeth of Baden (a marriage arranged by his parents when he was sixteen), he now shrugged off the depressing scenes of Palace affairs by making daily visits to Princess Marie Naryshkin. In no time, he had completely turned his back on his fair haired, quietly behaved wife, and spent almost all his time with Naryshkin.

Being the Tsar, his unfaithfulness in marriage and his lack of religious convictions made no difference to his having absolute control over the Russian Church. So, when a new "Archbishop of Canterbury" was required, he appointed a friend of his, Prince Galitsin—a rich young man, notorious for his outrageous public life and low standards.

As time went by, Alexander became more accustomed to being the all-powerful Tsar, and his self confidence grew. Very soon, his confidence developed into arrogance and conceit. Here he was, the tall, handsome Tsar, always resplendent in the dazzling uniform of the Royal Commander of the Imperial Army. Conscious of his striking appearance, he spent a great deal of time impressing the nobility, and when he became bored with that, he decided to widen his 'audience' by going into foreign affairs.

As one who hated the ambitions of Napoleon—Emperor of France and avowed conqueror of Europe—the young Tsar began stirring the Austrians and the Prussians to help him to withstand Napoleon. The brutality and brainlessness of the old Tsar had certainly been replaced with the adroit, subtle

Tsar Alexander

cunning of Alexander. He was in his element manipulating foreign powers, even to the extent of wresting five million pounds (a vast fortune then) from Britain to help him deal with the French. When it came to practical warfare, however, Alexander was very green. While he dreamed of leading his army to glory and being acclaimed the liberator of Europe, he did virtually nothing about the equipment, training and discipline of his troops. In fact, when Napoleon started a war against Austria, Alexander wasted time on a round of visits to various royal families making boastful predictions.

Eventually, the clash came when Russian and French forces confronted each other in 1806. The Russian army was headed by a cynical old general named Kutusov, who had already resigned himself to defeat. Alexander arrived on the scene just as hostilities began. With him, he brought muddle and confusion. It was his first and worst attempt at directing a military campaign. Somehow, he even became detached from his H.Q. and got lost, very narrowly escaping the final humiliation of capture by the French. In the end, he had to flee from the battlefield, knowing that his army was being utterly routed.

Alexander returned to St. Petersburg covered with shame. There, with his pride shattered and his dreams of glory lying in rags, he began to see the ugliness of his life—his conceit, his immorality, and his vain ambitions. And, as he brooded on these things, he began to be greatly troubled by something which had recently happened to his boyhood friend, Prince Galitsin. The prince, soon after Alexander had appointed him to the high office in the Russian Church, had began to feel acutely uncomfortable about his sinful way of life. He had begun to read the Gospels to see what they were all about. As he read, his eyes were opened, and he came to regard himself as a lost sinner in the sight of a holy God, resulting in an experience of conversion which changed his life completely.

Alexander was jarred by Galitsin's experience. The most abandoned, irreverent man from among his boyhood friends now talked about a living Saviour. One day Galitsin challenged the Tsar, saying, "Have you ever read the Gospels?"

"No," replied the Tsar, "I've heard bits in church, but I can't say that I've really read them. I've always been too busy."

Now, however, in the time of shame and derision, Alexander thought very much about Galitsin, and in the secrecy of his royal bedroom, he started to read his Bible. Soon, he was writing to Prince Galitsin, "This book which you put into my hands has opened up to me a new world." From that time, Galitsin became a regular visitor to the Palace, for Alexander had started to search for the meaning of life and eternity. But the search was to take him some time.

Time was something Alexander did not have. He had struck out at the lion Napoleon, and the day of reckoning was coming. Napoleon, following their first encounter, had gone on to devastate the Prussian army and had taken possession of Berlin. Alexander had no time to lose. He must stop

Napoleon soon, or in no time he would be on Russian soil. Hurriedly, the Tsar made his second attempt to defeat the lion of Europe. 120,000 Russian troops, supported by nearly 500 heavy guns, marched into Northern Poland where they struggled against the French for six months. But it all ended in dismal failure, and Alexander had to agree to talk peace with his enemy.

He met Napoleon in June 1807, on a sumptuous, specially built houseboat. To the amazement of the world, the two bitter antagonists seemed to become the closest of friends, so that what they arranged together was not merely an armistice, but a solid pact of unity to stand together against all enemies.

Alexander may possibly have entered into a great diplomatic lie to give him time to rebuild his army, and to plan a further offensive against Napoleon.

As the Tsar went on down life's pathway, personal tragedy brought him back to his search for God. His little daughter— the second and only surviving child born to Princess Elizabeth —developed tuberculosis and died. He had been unfaithful to his wife, but their sorrow brought them together again, and Alexander became more than ever aware that someone far greater than he held the keys to life and eternity.

Then, once again, the shadow of Napoleon fell across his reign. The French Emperor had decided to crush Austria, and he called upon Russia to fulfil the terms of their pact by providing troops to assist him. Alexander was dismayed. He had never expected to be held to his pact. There was no alternative but to mobilise an army to help the French, but the cunning Tsar took so long about it, that the French won their war unaided, and entered Vienna while the Russian troops were still crossing Poland—moving at a snail's pace and losing their way every few miles.

Once back home, Alexander began building a really large army in absolute secrecy. With his chiefs of staff, he planned for the day when he would deliberately draw the French onto Russian soil, and defeat them at last. But Napoleon was too shrewd. Realising that Alexander was not the naive young ruler he had seemed to be when they signed their agreement, and that he was a deceiver, Napoleon's fury was aroused. Within a year, the angry and determined French Emperor was leading his mighty army northwards—to Moscow.

As war approached, the Tsar found himself in a very different frame of mind than in previous years. Gone was the arrogant liberator of Europe, fighting for personal glory. In his place was an older man, very subdued, conscious of the grim cost of war, carrying a great weight of responsibility for the lives of his men, and fighting not for prestige, but for the ultimate defence of his people. As Napoleon drew near, Alexander turned to God in prayer. In the autumn of 1812, Napoleon arrived, and old General Kutusov tried to defend the road to Moscow at Borodino. For hours artillery roared ceaselessly, cavalry units charged, and foot soldiers in brilliant-coloured uniforms clashed in hand to hand fighting.

"Never did a battle cost the lives of so many generals and officers," wrote a French diplomat. Shattered by artillery, cut down by cavalry and bayoneted by infantry, the Russians stood firm, until General Kutusov gave the command to retreat. The French pursued.

At last, Napoleon breasted the Hill of Sparrows and saw before him in the distance, lit up by brilliant sunshine, the great domes and shining copper spires of Moscow. But inside the city, there was feverish activity as the entire population prepared to leave, taking as much as they could with them. Then they left it to Napoleon—a desolate and forlorn Moscow. There was no surrender by the city; there was no plea for terms. There was just nothing. And within hours of Napoleon's entry, the city was mostly in flames—either by the hand of Count Rostoptchin, Russian ex-Governor, or by accident.

In St. Petersburg, every noble family thought the war was lost and blamed the Tsar for the catastrophe. But for Alexander, the flames and death of Moscow, pride of Russia, was not only the beginning of victory, but it dawned on him as a vivid picture of what it means to become a Christian. When Alexander, with all his pomp, pride, self-love, pleasure, lusts and sin died to himself, then, and only then, would he really be able to come to Christ in repentance and faith.

"Except a corn of wheat fall into the ground and die, it abideth alone, but if it dies, it brings forth much fruit. He that loveth his life shall lose it; and he that hateth his life in this world shall keep it unto life eternal" (John 12:24).

Moscow burning

For the first time in his life, Alexander prayed prayers that God was ready to hear. For the first time, he was truly humbled and repentant, finding the truth of David's words, "a broken and a contrite heart, O God, thou wilt not despise" (Psalm 51). God answered his prayers, and from that moment, he was no longer a seeking soul, but a man who knew and walked with his Saviour.

Napoleon waited five weeks in Moscow for surrender. Twice he sent word to Alexander offering peace terms. But he heard nothing. Then, with his supplies finished, he led his army out of Moscow, to face almost total destruction by the terrible Russian winter. The Tsar took up his pen and wrote to his great friend and counsellor Prince Galitsin, "My faith is now sincere and ardent. It grows firmer every day and I taste joys of a kind I never knew before. For several years now, I have been seeking my way. The reading of the Scripture, which I know very superficially, has done me a benefit which is not possible to express in words. Pray to the Almighty Father, and to our Lord Jesus, and to the Spirit . . . that they may guide me and confirm me in the only way of salvation."

Immediately after Napoleon's failure in Russia, Alexander secured a treaty with Prussia and continued southwards to pursue him. Napoleon quickly assembled another large army and it took several great battles and Alexander's skill as a negotiator to bring other nations into the war, before Napoleon could be driven back onto his native soil.

Alexander called his generals together. Should they locate and destroy Napoleon's remaining army, or should they by-pass them and go straight for Paris? The generals disagreed and while they argued it out, the Tsar slipped out of the room.

"In my heart," he wrote afterwards, "I had an irresistable desire to place everything in the hands of God. The Council of War was still going on. I left it for a moment to retire to my room. Then I fell on my knees and poured out my heart to the Lord . . ." Soon, he returned to his generals to say, "My decision is taken—we shall march at once on Paris." Paris surrendered to Alexander in March 1814. There was no violence, no humiliation and no reprisals. Alexander was now a Christian as well as a military commander. All he sought was the removal of Napoleon to exile on the Isle of Elba, and then France could go free.

When Alexander returned to direct the affairs of his land, his whole way of life had become radically changed. Dr. Tarassar—his second physician—thought that he spent far too long every morning in prayer than was good for the health of his knees!

He was fully and completely reconciled to Princess Elizabeth and together they renounced the gross luxury and excesses of normal royal life, to live in a much plainer house with the minimum of attendants. They gave great support to the Bible Society of Russia, founded by Prince Galitsin to bring the Scriptures into the hands of the poor. In the last ten years of his reign, Alexander negotiated the famous 'Holy Alliance', established a university system in Russia with seven large colleges, founded a system of over 2,000 local schools and 200 gymnasia for the health of youth, emancipated the serfs of the Baltic provinces, set up a national corn storage plan for the relief of peasants in depression, and cut government expenditure sufficiently to abolish income tax.

Despite all this, he ruled over a backward and barbaric nation with no single minister of state who was worthy of his lofty aims and intentions. Behind his back, government officials practised injustice and tyranny, cultivating private corps of secret police and spies. The Tsar personally became the most kindly, feelingful ruler the Russian people had ever had. He moved freely among his people and knew particularly well the different congregations of Christians in his main cities—even down to a single family of evangelical Quakers worshipping in St. Petersburg.

The Christian Tsar died in 1825, having moved from arrogance and failure to repentance and success, proving the words of Scripture, "Humble yourselves, therefore, under the mighty hand of God, that He may exhalt you in due time (1 Peter, 5:6)".

Lieutenant Bowers, January 1911

BOWERS OF THE ANTARCTIC

Lieutenant "Birdie" Bowers

The name of Henry Bowers has an indelible place in the annals of exploration and discovery. Bowers was only twenty-eight when, with Captain Scott and Dr. 'Bill' Wilson, he lay down for the last time in a tiny tent caught in a swirling blizzard during March 1912, on the return journey from the South Pole. In the opinion of everyone, Bowers had been one of the outstanding men of the expedition. According to Scott, he always emerged as the fittest after the most gruelling physical ordeals. Wilson found him the most reliable. Sir George Green admired his amazing memory; and they all depended upon his irrepressible cheerfulness to keep them going through the very worst moments.

Bowers came from a tough, Scottish seafaring family. His father, Captain Alexander Bowers, had sailed race-winning clippers, and had penetrated further up the Yangtse-Kiang than any other Westerner. He had founded ports, and been a representative of the Indian Government in seeking to open up trade with Burma. But the active life of this generous, open-hearted captain was cut short by the rigours of the sea. He left behind two little girls, one little boy, and a sorrowing widow who eyed her son and hoped that he would never follow his father down to the sea.

Mrs. Bowers brought up her family in a large house in Sidcup. Every morning before breakfast, they sang a hymn (by Sankey), read a chapter from the Bible, and had prayers together. The children were brought up to know the meaning of the cross of Christ and to trust in Him. Their mother often told them how their father had lived and died a fervent Christian, but she never mentioned the sea, for fear that the seed of desire might be planted in young Henry's heart. One

19

morning, however, Mrs. Bowers walked into Henry's bedroom, and saw pinned up over his bed a large picture of a ship in full sail. In that moment, her worst fears were realised. She knew that her boy would follow his father.

It was a great act of motherly self-sacrifice which took Mrs. Bowers to the naval training school H.M.S. Worcester, to have Henry admitted as a cadet. He was fourteen, a short stocky boy, with a wild shock of reddish hair and a very prominent, beak-like nose.

The routine of H.M.S. Worcester was vastly different from that of a grammar school. Scrubbing, swabbing, and cleaning ship were the basic ingredients, along with strenuous activities designed to harden boys into officer material for large sailing vessels. In the long dormitories below deck, Bowers got a reputation as 'the best tempered boy in the world'. His best friend on the ship remembered him as "the strongest and best character I have ever known. It was his never failing practice, during the whole time he was aboard the Worcester, to sit at one of the school desks on the main deck—before the whole ship's company—and read his Bible for a quarter of an hour every evening, during the time that we used to set apart for 'slewing round'."

Bowers passed out of the Worcester at sixteen, with top grade passes in his theory and seamanship examinations, and started his practical apprenticeship in the merchant navy by joining a four masted barque, the Loch Torridon. In this massive windjammer, just before the turn of the century, the excited young apprentice set out on his first voyage to Australia. Sharing a cabin with another trainee, he found himself constantly on duty. "Work never stops," he wrote home, and it didn't. When he was not performing the naval ritual of scrubbing and painting, he was assigned to the acting mate to learn navigation. The captain was a terrifying figure, with steel-grey eyes that could wither up the most hardened seamen who came up against him. The apprentices' cabin was a kind of hut, built on the main deck, which played host to every wave that ventured on board. When the seas were running high, everything the boys had was afloat. But they were still proud of their ship, because it could pass almost everything else under sail.

The 'Terra Nova' held up in the ice pack

Bowers himself made outstanding progress, even winning the esteem of his notoriously hard-to-please skipper. He was eighteen, and still only an apprentice when the captain made him third mate, with authority over the crew. It was his third voyage to Australia and things were not easy for him, as the Loch Torridon crew hated their captain and were only too ready to vent their feelings on a raw, inexperienced junior officer.

Matters grew even worse when the first mate, after a fearful row with the captain, stalked off to his cabin and remained there for the rest of the voyage. At the same time, the second mate went sick, so Bowers found himself in the position of first officer under the captain. Storms in the South Atlantic saw him up aloft, high in the swaying rigging, leading the work of making fast huge sails. When day after day passed with wretched ocean mists enshrouding relentless driving rain, it was Bowers who had to hold up the morale of a miserable crew. Nearness to the Antarctic circle found him at the ship's rail, listening to the cries of seabirds—penguins perhaps—with a strange longing to be with those early polar explorers who were so much in the news.

"This has not been an easy voyage," he wrote home. "It seems splendid to be made third mate, and a big step after only two years an apprentice . . . but the skipper is out against his officers and is difficult to get on with." With his life filled with the activity and responsibility of being acting first mate, Bowers began to let his mind feast on his ambitions. The world was a wonderful place, he mused, and his opportunities seemed limitless. Yet at the same time, he found himself shuddering at the seamy side, the rottenness of the world, as he rubbed shoulders constantly with men who would have been expelled from anywhere except a prison or a merchant ship. When the Loch Torridon docked at Adelaide, he wrote, "The steward has deserted; we are getting ready for sea again. I went up to the city to extract the cook from jail, and brought him aboard in the afternoon. We are getting our new crew dumped aboard—all drunk."

His mind raced through ambitions and doubts together. "I must get on," he thought. Was the world really so much a fallen world as he had grown up to believe? Would only those people who trusted in a Saviour and lived to serve Him be saved? Even while Bowers wrestled with his thoughts, he had to prepare his ship for the return journey round the Horn, and home. All hands were called, the anchor hauled up, the sails set, and the great steel-hulled windjammer was off again. With the flurry of activity over and the ship on a steady course, the acting first mate returned to his spiritual struggle; on the one side—the world; on the other side—the unseen Lord Jesus who, Bowers believed, had so loved him as to die on a bitter cross to bear the punishment of his sins.

"I seemed to get into a quagmire of doubts and disbeliefs. Why should we have so many disappointments when life is hard enough without them? Everything seems a hopeless problem. I felt I should never get out, there was no purpose in it." Suddenly, the Lord Himself seemed to step in.

"One night on deck, when things were at their blackest, it seemed to me that Christ came to me and showed me why we are here, and what the purpose of life really is. It is to make a great decision—to choose between the material and the spiritual. While just on the point of choosing the world for good, a possibility which my early training had long kept at bay, Christ revealed himself to me. Not in a vision; not after hearing emotional preaching, but away at sea. Beside Him, the world at its best was nothing, not even life itself. He filled my whole horizon . . . who could refuse to stick up for such a friend, who even knew him afar off?"

"It is very difficult to express in words what I suddenly saw so plainly, and it is sometimes difficult to recapture it myself. I know too that my powerful ambitions to get on in this world will conflict with that pure light that I saw for a moment, but I can never forget that I did realise, in a flash, that nothing which happens to our bodies really matters." Ever afterwards, Bowers looked back upon this intense experience as the time when the Lord met with him, a weak believer, to confirm him in the trust of his childhood, and to lead him on.

He had one more voyage in the Loch Torridon before leaving sail for steam, a voyage which broke all records to make the fastest Pacific crossing for sixteen years. Then he joined the S.S. Cape Breton bound for New York. It was not as good a post as he hoped for, but by now Bowers clearly felt the unseen hand on his life. In advising his sister about her future, he wrote: "Are you finding, like I did, that taking too much thought for the future only makes disappointment worse? As I have had enough of taking my future into my own hands, I will just leave everything to the One Who knows my ultimate end already." Bowers was in New York, aged twenty-one, and still serving on the S.S. Cape Breton, when he received a telegram telling him that he had been gazetted as a sub-lieutenant to the Royal Indian Marine Service. It was a coveted distinction to be transferred from the merchant service to the R.I.M.S., and Bowers knew that the Commandant of H.M.S. Worcester, his old training ship, must have arranged it.

When he returned to England, he went straight to the Worcester to express his gratitude, and while there, was introduced to Sir Clements Markham, the 'father' of Captain Scott's Discovery expedition. The Commandant turned to Sir Clements and indicating Bowers said, "Here is a man who will be leading one of those expeditions some day." Sir Clements looked long and hard at the young officer. The remark lodged deeply in his mind.

The Indian navy was a far cry from windjammers battling round the Horn, or smoky steamers churning their way across the Atlantic. Bowers found himself posted to a shallow-bottomed gunboat patrolling the Irrawaddy River. Here, ships anchored by tying up to trees, and depended on the vigilant steering of officers who knew every bend and whirlpool in the river. Clouds of mosquitoes hovered everywhere and the climate was like a furnace. One advantage of service on the Irrawaddy was the opportunity it gave Bowers to go ashore, where he cycled up mountains to the Chinese border, watched big game in the jungle, found gold in a mountain stream, learned Hindustani, and set himself to master every sporting activity he could. Not surprisingly, he proved too musclebound to play squash.

In the same way as he had gained early responsibility on the Loch Torridon, so he obtained it in the Indian navy. A chain of unusual events led him to the command of the R.I.M.S. Bhamo, a 200-feet gunboat which was generally

On the Beardmore Glacier

regarded as the most difficult ship to handle in the entire fleet. Bowers took the place of a lieutenant-commander so successfully that he became known as 'the comet'. A fanatic for physical fitness, his work output was quite incredible, but he was inwardly far from self-sufficient. "I have so often called upon God's help in an extremity when nothing more could be done by me, that these things can never be forgotten. I know that I am often blinded to the things eternal in the rush and strenuousness of life; still, I trust that I shall never let go." In off-duty weekends ashore, he would always be found at Sunday services. Once, after attending a seamens' service in Calcutta, he wrote home, "The Sankey hymns were

really splendid. What good old memories of Sidcup they
bring back to me! I always thank God for those morning
hymns we used to have together before breakfast. They are
indelibly printed on my memory."

For nearly a year, Mrs. Bowers had her son on leave at
home, now back in Scotland. Then he was appointed to
H.M.S. Fox, a British naval cruiser carrying five-inch guns,
operating in the Persian Gulf, the hottest climate in the
world. Bowers was busy chasing dhows engaged in gun-run-
ning when suddenly in 1910, he was summoned to Bombay
to see the Director of the Royal Indian Marine Service.
Apprehensively, he stepped inside his Chief's thickly carpeted
office, wondering what he had done wrong. The Director
greeted him quietly, and held up two telegrams. "Lt. Bowers
services requisitioned for the Antarctic if he can be spared."
And: "If he can be in London by May 15th, he will be
appointed." The Commandant of H.M.S. Worcester and Sir
Clements Markham had placed his credentials and records of
service before Captain Scott who, without even a formal
application or an interview, passed over 8,000 applicants and
cabled Bombay to secure his services. Bowers gasped in
amazement and felt convinced that under such remarkable
circumstances, God was overruling the course of his life.

The Terra Nova, Captain Scott's expedition ship, left
Britain in June 1910, with Bowers in charge of all the stores.
Very soon, he was standing out as one of the exceptional
men of the team. Bowers wrote, "The person who has most
impressed me among us is Dr. Wilson . . . I am sure he is a real
Christian, there is no mistaking it, it comes out in everything
. . . he is a wonderful artist too." Dr. Wilson had also made a
private note about Bowers: "A short, redheaded, thick set
little man with a very large nose, is a perfect model of effi-
ciency, but in addition to this, he has the most unselfish
character I have ever met in a man anywhere."

In no time, his nose had earned him the nickname 'Birdie',
and the party had mutually decided that there should be a
'Mount Birdie' somewhere in the Antarctic. Frequently,
Bowers was called into consultation with Scott, who became
so impressed with him, that he decided to take him ashore
on the landing party. In January 1911, the landing party

disembarked from the Terra Nova at Cape Evans, to prepare for the South Pole venture. "Every day," said Scott, "Bowers conceives or carries out some plan to benefit the camp . . . I have never seen anyone so unaffected by the cold." As the expedition progressed, Bowers and Wilson were the principal morale-boosters. Griffith Taylor recalled that Bowers was always bringing specimens of rock to the geologist with some remark like, "Here you are: here's a gabroid nodule impaled in basalt with felspar and olivant rampant." Ponting, the photographer, said, "No more cheery, joyful soul ever lived than he, nor any more disdainful of hardship . . . from the hour we disembarked in the South, he was Scott's privy councillor in all matters relating to the important work of provisioning the various exploring parties." The team continually met with shocks, setbacks, injuries; loss of motors, ponies, dogs; and terrible weather conditions. Scott paid even greater tribute to Bowers' "astonishing physique which enables him to continue to work under conditions which are absolutely paralysing to others . . . his intelligence is of quite a high order and his memory for details most exceptional."

On 18th January 1912, a party of five reached the South Pole - Scott, Wilson, Bowers, Oates and Evans. "We have fixed the exact spot of the South Pole," wrote Bowers, "and left the British Flag there. I have had the honour to be the observer, in fact I have navigated the party here and done all the observations since Teddy Evans returned. Amundsen's people left a tent with some of their discarded gear close to the Pole. They were here exactly a month ago. I am awfully sorry for Captain Scott who has taken the blow very well indeed."

On the way back from the Pole, troubles slowly closed in around the little party, and following the agonizing descent of the Beardmore Glacier in February, Evans collapsed and died. "We can't go on like this," wrote Scott a little later. "I don't know what I should do if Wilson and Bowers were not so determinedly cheerful about things." In March, Oates, who was in great pain, walked out into the blizzard and was not seen again. By now, death seemed inevitable for all of them, and Scott wrote, "Had we lived, I should have had a tale to tell . . . the end cannot be far."

Soon, he took up his pen again to write to Mrs. Bowers: "My dear Mrs. Bowers, I am afraid this will reach you after one of the heaviest blows of your life. I write when we are very near the end of our journey and I am finishing it in company with two gallant, noble gentlemen. One of these is your son. He has come to be one of my closest and soundest friends and I appreciate his wonderful upright nature, his ability and energy. As the troubles have thickened, his dauntless spirit ever shone brighter and he has remained cheerful, hopeful and indomitable to the end. . . To the end, he talked of you and his sisters. One sees what a happy home he must have had . . ."

Bowers had no fear of death, for he faced it knowing the Friend of his father; the Friend his mother had introduced him to as a boy. His last words were written, probably on March 22nd 1912: --

Blizzard Camp,
11′ S of 1 Ton Depot.

'My own dearest mother,
    As this may be my last letter to you, I am sorry it is just
a short scribble. I have written little since we left the Pole,
but it has not been for want of thinking of you and the dear
girls. We have had a terrible journey back . . . God alone
knows what will be the outcome of the 22 miles march we
have to make, but my trust is still in Him and in the abound-
ing grace of my Lord and Saviour whom you brought me up
to trust in, and Who has been my stay through life. In His
keeping I leave you, and am only glad that I am permitted to
struggle on to the end . . . "
    Possibly within a few hours, Lieutenant Henry Bowers had
passed over the threshhold of eternity.

DISCOVERER OF CHLOROFORM

Sir James Simpson

Twenty-five miles from Edinburgh, on the road to Glasgow, is the town of Bathgate. In 1811, it was a small and casual village, where cows wandered up and down the high street with children playing round them. Only occasionally were they pushed aside to allow a coach and horses to clatter through. The village baker's shop was run by David Simpson and his wife, who had a hard time making ends meet for their daughter and six sons. In fact, they had only just steered clear of bankruptcy when their seventh 'great event' came, and the village doctor delivered James Simpson for a fee of 10s.6d.

James Simpson was only nine years old when his mother died, leaving his elder sister to take up the household reins. The children grew up very poor, but very closely-knit as a family. Simpson became a rugged, stocky sort of boy with a taste for anything vigorous, but he also had a flair for books. By thirteen, he was clearly the scholar of the family and the others decided to make him 'their' student and to support him at college.

So in 1825, Edinburgh University gained another hard-up student, fourteen-year-old Simpson. Two years of study sped by and Simpson decided to start a medical course. The medical students worked in the Edinburgh Royal Infirmary where, on the top floor, was one of the most famous operating theatres of the day: famous because Robert Liston was the surgeon, and Liston was the man who could amputate a limb faster than anyone else.

On his first day as a medical student, Simpson took his place with the spectators round the operating table. There were no white tiles, gowns or masks in those days. Even worse, there were no anaesthetics. A patient with frightened, staring eyes was brought into the room and laid on the table. The assistants held her down firmly and a bowl was put in the right place to catch the blood. Then Liston, his black, gentlemen's suit protected only by a small apron, took up his knife. Simpson watched, taut and horrified, as Liston plunged the knife into his patient. Terrifying screams rent the air and buried deep into the mind of Simpson a longing to see the end of suffering, conscious surgery.

So brief was the medical training in those days, that Simpson qualified as an M.R.C.S. at eighteen. For a time, he assisted the village doctor at Bathgate, then he returned to Edinburgh to take his doctor of medicine degree and to stay as an assistant member of the hospital staff. He earned £50 a year and took every opportunity for research work. In fact, he spent his entire energies on getting honours, and they soon came his way. Because of the success of his research work, he was elected the Senior President of the Royal Medical Society of Edinburgh when he was only twenty-four. But even while the laurels were piling up, he was beginning to feel an undercurrent of dissatisfaction and unrest in his life.

"Yesterday was my twenty-sixth birthday and what a fearful waste of time is summed up in that little numeral . . . it is awful to think how such a small fraction of time out of these twenty-six years has been employed as it ought to have been. I am always sad on my birthday and yesterday sadder than ever. It was one of those days—those fitful days of gloom—in which the past appeared to me as almost lost—the future as a labyrinth of vexation and disappointment."

Simpson was asking himself, "What is life for?" but his hopes and ambitions were too active for these great questions of life to bite home for long. He believed in this world and he believed that his work would win success and happiness. That was all there was to it.

It is amazing how much work Simpson packed into his early life to win success. Aged only twenty-seven, he became a lecturer at the University. His lectures (in obstetrics) were brilliant, his illustrations unique and his personality magnetic. The word went round and the students crowded into his lecture room. Simpson found himself with more money and a fast growing reputation. He was fed up with the life of a

A hospital ward in Simpson's day

lodger and he looked around for a house of his own. In Queen Street, he found a tall, elegant house to let and he took it. He furnished the downstairs rooms as consulting rooms and received private patients there. Even the tradesmen in the city began to take notice as hotel keepers and others found their businesses benefiting from the large numbers of wealthy people who visited Edinburgh just to consult Simpson.

Then came an even greater leap ahead for Simpson. In 1839, the old professor of midwifery at the University died and the post became vacant. The ambitious young Simpson wanted that post very badly, but he was not the only applicant and a very fierce battle lay before him. He set about finding sixty doctors to write him testimonials. Then he had two main

B

obstacles to get over. He was only twenty-eight, and more important, he was a bachelor, which would have disqualified him. Now it so happened that he had been in love with a Liverpool girl for some time, and he wrote to her saying, "My dear Jessie, within the last few days I have drawn out a formal application for a professorial chair . . . I write to make formal application for a wife." Jessie consented, and to the consternation of his opponents, Simpson ceased to be a bachelor. The great selection day came and the University Council met together. The representatives from the City Council (all tradesmen) supported the blue-eyed Simpson. The academic members were not at all enthusiastic about a mere baker's son, and they supported Dr. Kennedy, his rival. The vote was taken and Simpson won by seventeen votes to sixteen. He wrote home, "My dear mother. Jessie's honeymoon and mine is to begin tomorrow. I was elected professor today by a majority of one."

Simpson's appointment stirred up a great deal of jealousy. "Basking in sunny shallows," wrote one person, "was not Simpson's lot. He was seldom out of some big war or skirmish." As for the students and private patients, they thought more of Simpson than ever. At thirty-one, he was earning £4,000 a year in fees, and Jessie Simpson was pouring out more tea than any other woman in Edinburgh.

Outwardly, Simpson followed the Christian faith. He attended St. Stephen's Church, Edinburgh, where Dr. Muir preached evangelical sermons. But his real opinion of Christianity was 'good at death but not in life'. One day he returned home from lectures to find his little daughter seriously ill. No amount of treatment seemed to help her, and she rapidly deteriorated. When she died, her father was stunned and jarred into anguish. How pointless and cruel life seemed. Was there a life after death? Once again his mind asked many questions. But once again the buoyant spirits of the man with so much faith in the world carried him back to his work and ambitions. Simpson never studied the point and meaning of life so much as he studied the material things immediately around him.

Then, one day in 1846, the news came from America that a successful anaesthetic had been discovered. The discovery was a substance called ether. Within months, Robert Liston had tried it in Scotland. But the dangers and disadvantages of ether were very great and a more satisfactory anaesthetic had to be found. Simpson leapt into the struggle to find the answer, and through the summer and autumn of 1846 he and his helpers tried drug after drug, sniffing them, and recording the effects on themselves. Then came chloroform. A local chemist had suggested it but had not got round to producing a bottle. With typical impatience, Simpson obtained some from another town, but when he examined it, he shook his head dubiously. "After seeing such an unvolatile liquid, I despaired of it." The bottle lay untouched for a few days until one evening, Simpson decided to try it as a long shot. His helpers, Dr. Duncan and Dr. Keith, got out three tumblers and Simpson poured a little into each one. Then they breathed the fumes deeply. For a moment there was no effect, then Dr. Keith began laughing loudly. Duncan danced round the room like a child and Simpson felt very, very drunk. Suddenly, all three lost their senses and collapsed. They had found their 'better anaesthetic' and it became a tremendous success.

Simpson first tried chloroform for a mother in labour. She was so excited about the less painful birth that she named her baby girl Anaesthesia!

Simpson's brains and learning had brought him status and admiration. His tremendous rate of working had brought him a fortune. Now, his discovery of chloroform as an anaesthetic brought him national fame. And yet, Simpson felt as though he had been running away from life rather than succeeding in it. Those niggling questions of early life, those moments of wanting to know the meaning of it all—they were still there. He still had to answer them.

Certain people attacked anaesthetics on 'religious' grounds and Dr. Simpson published a reply based upon Scripture. It earned him the title 'Christian Physician.' but he knew in his heart that the description was false. He knew that really he worshipped success and secretly snubbed God under a cloak of Christian respectability.

Then came the death of his closest friend, Dr. John Reid. This man had been converted to the Lord Jesus Christ while alone in the Cumberland countryside, and Simpson had undoubtedly heard about it often. Simpson had watched

when Dr. Reid was suffering the intense pain of his last illness.
He had noticed his extraordinary peace. He had heard him
praying aloud to his Saviour. He had heard his dying words,
"The world is behind." And James Simpson, whose life
depended on this world and the things in it, could not forget
what he had seen and heard.

A new era was dawning for Dr. Simpson as he searched for
the answers to his spiritual questions. "I seldom saw him,"
said Dr. Dun, "without being asked the meaning of some
passage of Scripture."

Dr. Reid had known Christ in a personal way and Simpson
began searching for that same relationship. He started trying
to find a foothold in God's kingdom by his own efforts. His
churchgoing friends were quite startled when he offered to
help them in things they were doing for the Church. But the
time was drawing near when he would understand that the
only way to find Christ was to respond to the simple invitation, "Believe on the Lord Jesus Christ and thou shalt be
saved."

One day, Dr. Simpson was called to the bedside of an
invalid woman who was a firm Christian believer. As he
prescribed a course of treatment, she spoke to him about his
soul, and afterwards, he was moved to write to her asking for
daily prayer. In her reply, his patient challenged him about
the spiritual poverty of his rich life, so full of earthly achievement. She wrote, putting these words into his mouth:

"When benevolence shall have run its course, when there
shall be no sick to heal, no disease to cure, when all I have
been engaged about comes to a dead stop—WHAT is to fill
this heart and thought and powers of mine?"

Simpson had asked that question for years, but never faced
up to it. Now, he was acutely aware of the sinfulness of a life
which had been one long snub to Almighty God. A battle
raged within him. He was addicted to wealth and honours, but
he longed for forgiveness and knowledge of God. At last, his
struggles came to a head and he found his way to the house of
his invalid friend, saying, "I felt I must go somewhere tonight
. . . I wish to come to Christ, but I can't see Him."

The famous doctor was urged to repent of his sins before
God and to trust only upon Christ's death for salvation. No

Chloroform tested

one who earnestly seeks Christ in repentance is ever turned away, and by Christmas 1858, James Simpson knew that he was a changed man—a new Christian.

Simpson's conversion caused a considerable stir at the Royal Infirmary. Some of his friends were astonished. One said, "What a curious psychological phenomenon this step of Simpson's is! I can't make it out."

In his lecture room, Simpson told his students about his experience and called himself the oldest sinner and the youngest believer in the room. What difference had his conversion made to him? He told his students.

"In Christ," he said, "you will find a Saviour, a companion, a counsellor, a friend, a brother who loves you with a love greater than the human heart can conceive."

Life became utterly changed. Before conversion, he was entirely in the hands of this passing world. He loved it and lived for it, and he brought up his children to admire it and succeed in it. For a man of science and broad vision, his outlook had been so narrowly limited to material things. But now he was living in a new realm. He had been given a new start and was concerned about pleasing God. He became anxious that his children should all have the true riches and know Christ also. He ceased to involve himself in his chief sport—petty wrangles and disputes in the medical world. He became an earnest man, seeking the spiritual welfare of others.

Towards the end of his life, when he was in his fifties, Simpson was honoured with a knighthood. He had contributed greatly to the advance of anaesthetics by discovering the suitability of chloroform, and it was his strong advocacy that won its approval (even to the extent of gaining the confidence of Queen Victoria who bore Prince Leopold under chloroform—attended by James Simpson). He had laid the groundwork for the advanced study of gynaecology, and some of his written work continued to be the finest exposition of the subject for the best part of a century. Despite all this, when he was asked at a great public meeting what his greatest discovery had been, he replied, without any hesitation, "That I have a Saviour."

Sir James Young Simpson died aged 58. On the day of his funeral, no work was done in Edinburgh and 2,000 people followed the hearse. His words of witness had become very familiar in Scottish circles:—

"We can do nothing to wash away our guilt before God but Christ has done all that is required. Believe on the Lord Jesus Christ and thou shalt be saved."

THE WORLD'S MOST NOTORIOUS COUNTERFEITER

Alves Reis

Alves Reis was easily the richest man in Portugal. He had risen from bankruptcy to multi-millionaire status in the space of only two years—success which came to him by courtesy of a famous firm of London banknote printers. They supplied him with a fortune in 'genuine' counterfeit notes, as the unwitting victims of the world's most incredible fraud.

It was a crime which almost enabled its author to take over the national Bank of Portugal. When it was uncovered (by chance, in 1925), it rocked the nation, led to the disgrace of leading public figures, and toppled the government.

Reis started out in life governed by a materialism and ambition which made fraud as necessary as everyday speech. After his first year as an engineering student, he abandoned his course to get married and emigrated to the emerging Portuguese colony of Angola.

"I was twenty-one years old, of a romantic temperament and given to dreaming great things. My short life had already led me through labyrinths of passion and fantastic visions. The selfish and sensual materialism of the times had taught me to oppose all spiritual theories and to seek material wealth."

In his pocket, Reis carried a most impressive document. It was a diploma in engineering science granted by an imaginary "Polytechnic School of Engineering" at Oxford. With this forged, English degree, Reis made astonishing progress in Angola. By the age of twenty-three, he had become the colony's top scientific civil servant as well as the 'Dr. Beeching' of the Railways. Before very long, Reis decided that a life bonded to a state-employer was not for him. It was time he became a millionaire. So he resigned his position and

39

There was no shortage of passengers on Reis' new Angola Railways!

formed a highly successful trading company. Within three years, he had moved his headquarters to a prestige suite of offices in Lisbon, and ran a chauffeur-driven Nash sedan car.

Full of self-confidence, Reis dreamed of becoming the Cecil Rhodes of Angola, planning and financing great schemes for development and colonisation. But in the world of the early 1920's, a financial crisis hit the colony which threatened to wreck all his plans. Reis had to find capital quickly. He found it by taking over the entire Royal Trans-Africa Railway Company (of Angola); as Managing Director, he could swindle the company of the money he needed. Despite his cunning, the manouevre was doomed to failure and led Reis to a damp, dark Oporto prison; there was a formidable list of charges to face. But Alves Reis was becoming a master-criminal. He paid friends to spread the news that he

was the victim of a political plot; he paid lawyers to manipu-
late the charges, and with a few deft 'adjustments' to his
company's affairs, he was a free man. To garnish his triumph,
he made sure that his accusers ended up in worse trouble
themselves.

The fifty-five days spent in prison had not, however,
passed without some effect on the young financier. It was
not the effect the law intended. Sitting day after day in his
cell, Reis thought long and hard about his great plans for
Angola. He knew the mighty rivers, the cheap native labour,
the vast mineral resources, and the great 'tablelands', with
their rich vegetation and perfect climate for wealthy, European
colonialists. Alves Reis would develop it all. "How can I do
it," he thought. "Even if I secure my acquittal, my name and
my money is lost."

As he thought, he conceived an incredible plan. Portuguese
currency had long since left the gold standard. The Bank of
Portugal made no attempt to back every banknote with solid
gold in the vaults. Whenever the government needed money,
without any fuss or 'devaluation', they simply printed more
banknotes. Just one precaution was taken. So that the general
public should not know that money was losing its value, the
new banknotes were issued in great secrecy. This was the key
to Reis's plan. He would assume the position of an appointed
agent of the Angola government to arrange a secret issue of
banknotes. He selected his henchmen, all of whom would be
highly reputable, rich men, convinced that he was acting
officially.

No sooner was he out of prison than Reis began putting
his plan into operation. After his office staff had gone home,
he worked late into the evenings forging a contract between
the Angola government and himself. The contract required
Reis to get a vast sum of money invested in Angola by
outside financiers. In exchange, he would have the right and
the responsibility of arranging a secret banknote issue—
together with the proceeds. Such a contract would seem
plausible to the men whose help he needed. Angola was
desperately short of capital—and it would explain how Reis—
a private financier—should be given the job of handling
official currency.

He got the contract legally authorised—as all Portuguese contracts must be—without it being read by the official, and forged onto it all the necessary signatures. Then he was ready to bring in his associates. Karel Marang was a Dutch diplomat and a financier. Adolf Hennis was a very wealthy German businessman. They were both intrigued and excited by the idea of lending money to Angola in return for arranging the printing and distribution of banknotes, for they were bound to make a considerable amount of money. It was Marang who travelled to London to arrange the printing of the notes. On December 4th 1924, he stepped into the imposing office of Sir William Waterlow, head of the famous firm of money and postage-stamp printers. Waterlows were the official printers of 500-escudos notes for Portugal (£5 notes).

Sir William, completely taken in by Reis's fake contract which Marang showed him, agreed to print 200,000 notes (to start with) and to keep strict secrecy. The bill for a million pounds-worth of money would be £1,500! The notes would, of course, be printed from the official plates which Waterlows already had in their possession and the order confirmed by a personal letter sent to Sir William from the Governor of the Bank of Portugal—or rather from Alves Reis.

In February 1925, Marang collected the first consignment of banknotes, packed in a suitcase, and caught the Liverpool Street boat train to Harwich. Being a diplomat as well as a financier, his bags carried the orange labels of the diplomatic service, so there was nothing to fear from the customs. Soon, the notes were being spread across Portugal by Alves Reis and his agents. As time passed and more banknotes were delivered, Reis and his colleagues founded the Bank of Angola to help distribute notes, and to arrange investments in the colony. Reis's big schemes began to take shape. "I formed a number of companies," he wrote, "and I approached the government with a plan for colonisation of the centre-land. I also made a contract with the High Commissioner to build an important new railway line." For himself, Reis bought the most expensive mansion in Lisbon, the Golden Boy Palace, and he gave his wife a fortune in jewellery.

Thousands upon thousands of green 500-escudos notes continued to be changed by Reis's agents. Banks round the

One of the banknotes fraudulently issued by Reis in 1925.

Reis lived in a fabulous mansion in the heart of Lisbon.

world were soon holding vast sums in his name, and he was hailed as the great financial genius who was elevating the nation out of economic stagnation. Many times, bank managers grew deeply suspicious of the endless bundles of crisp new banknotes passing through their hands. Frequently, they referred samples to the official experts at Lisbon. Were they genuine? Of course they were. They were printed on the Bank of Portugal's own plates.

By the time Waterlows had printed notes worth three million pounds, Reis was Portugal's richest man, practically owned Angola, and was buying up the shares of the Bank of Portugal. Soon, he would own the very bank whose notes he was forging, then he would be high and dry from detection. But Reis had not bargained for the interference of the press. A leading daily paper in Lisbon, incensed by the extravagance and indulgent luxuries of Reis and his colleagues, began to suspect some enormous swindle. The paper opened a violent campaign against the activities of the Bank of Angola. Then, one day, Bank of Portugal inspectors swooped on a branch of Reis's bank to find one great flaw in the banknotes which **had** so long deceived them. The notes were perfect, but the **serial** numbers were exactly the same as notes which had been printed some years previously.

Within hours, the whole fabric of fraud collapsed. Reis and others were arrested and taken to Lisbon. Panic seized the country as the news got round that thousands of useless notes were in circulation. There was a stampede to the Bank of Portugal as crowds of people rushed to change their 500-escudos notes. For Reis, it was to be the fight of his life. "Determined not to be overcome, I attacked innocent people. I falsely accused the Bank of Portugal, the High Commissioner, politicians and financiers. I attempted to involve them all."

Almost unanimously, the Portuguese nation affirmed that their leaders had authorised a secret issue of banknotes, and were now making Reis their scapegoat. More than twenty important people were arrested. Reis, from his prison, hired the best lawyers and continued to implicate others in his crimes. The government in the meantime passed new laws increasing the prison sentences for fraud. It took six years to clear away the debris of lies and false trails spread by Reis, before the prosecution was ready for a trial. At last, worn out, penniless, and deserted by everyone, Reis swallowed a phial of deadly poison which he had kept during his six years remand. Even that failed, and he regained consciousness to find himself in the prison hospital.

A few beds away from Reis lay a sick prisoner who had become deeply affected by reading the Bible. Reis recalled later: "He sought to prove to me that the Bible is God's Book. We had heated discussions. A conceited desire to prove my point of view led me to read parts of the Bible. I came across the definite assertion, 'Search the Scriptures; for in them you think you have eternal life, and these are they which testify of me.' I then made a systematic, but merely intellectual study of the Bible. I was coldly critical, yet I was surprised to have to arrive at the conclusion that Christ can be traced in the Scriptures from Genesis to Revelation. He is there as the Saviour, the promise of whose coming runs right through the Old Testament. My mind became very concerned with the authenticity of the Bible."

Reis began to worry very much about the existence of God. He wrote to an old friend who was a priest and a scholar in the Roman Catholic Church, and began to receive advice. Still, the matter of his 'innocence' had to be settled. Fresh forgeries were prepared for him which would prove once and for all that the Directors of the Bank of Portugal were his employers. This time, the forgeries were accompanied by fervent prayers to God for their success! But instead of success, Reis was seized with a strange compulsion. He did not want it; indeed, he fought desperately against it, but he could not shake it off. It was a compulsion to confess his crimes.

Reis yielded. Firstly, he followed the urging of his friend to join the Church of Rome. Then, after six long years of remand, he stood trial alongside seven associates, and his poor wife. For five hours, Reis made legal history with a speech of confession before the court. Fervently, he sought to demonstrate the innocence of his confederates, but all except one were sentenced. Reis was given twenty-five years penal servitude. Up till then, he had been on remand—wearing his own clothes and with many liberties within the prison. Now, he would be alone in a cell, his hair cropped, clad in a convict's uniform, and known by a number.

Back inside the grim walls of the Cadeva Nacional, he was tormented night and day by his conscience because of the sentences passed on his innocent dupes. In his anguish, he seized the Bible which had lain untouched since his first study in the hospital. What could it tell him?

"The Scriptures opened up to me new horizons. The Epistle to the Romans taught me justification by faith, and Hebrews overthrew my views on the priesthood. All I had read by teachers of the Roman Church was so different from what I seemed to find in the Scriptures. Who could assist me in my studies? I prayed unceasingly, seeking light from God. My progress was slow and I was afraid of relapsing to rationalism. I knew of no group of Christians like those depicted in the New Testament. I read in the Bible, 'Call upon Me in the day of trouble: I will deliver you.' By His grace, the Lord sent me deliverance."

In 1931, Reis received through the post a bundle of evangelical tracts, sent to him on impulse by a Christian. "On each of the tracts, which I still treasure, I read, 'Anyone seeking information may receive free help by writing to George Howes'." Reis wrote the same day. Mr. Howes was a Brethren Missionary working in Portugal. He visited the notorious criminal and placed at his disposal all his books. It was while reading an article given him by George Howes that Reis came fully to understand conversion and he passed through the experience of being reconciled to Christ. "I read and re-read that article, and my soul vibrated with profound and irrepressible joy."

The inveterate liar, the impossible fraud, the uncontrollable egotist—Alves Reis, began to be transformed in an amazing way by his encounter with God. Even solitary confinement became a place of peace and power.

"In the oppressive silence my spirit was asphyxiated, whilst dormant fleshly lusts and passions were aroused. The only solace was to fall on my knees and seek help from the One of whom Paul the prisoner said, 'I can do all things through Christ who strengthens me'."

Influenced by the great change which came over Reis, one of his confederates in prison (Adriano Silva) also began to seek God, and eventually became a convinced Christian. Then, as the result of many letters and visits, Reis's wife and eldest son came under the influence of his changed life, to experience for themselves the power and love of Christ. As time went by, the former criminal became a trusted prisoner and was almost a missioner among the hundreds of convicts. He worked on revising Portuguese tracts, and contributing to a regular Christian magazine.

Alves Reis became a free man again in 1945, after serving 19½ years of his sentence. He helped his three sons in their struggling import and export business and served a dozen evangelical churches in Lisbon as a lay preacher. Ten years later he died, a poor, but happy man. He died knowing a Saviour. He died forgiven by God. He died in the knowledge that he had led others to the Lord. And he died leaving three sons all active in the service of Christ.

The fiddler in action

THE STORY OF "FIDDLER JOSS"

Joshua Poole

However tough the law has been, or however complex the medical treatment, our ingenuity has never solved the problems of alcoholism and drug addiction. Yet the Christian Church has seen countless cases of hopeless and notorious victims utterly transformed by the Gospel message.

"Fiddler Joss" underwent this kind of change. His early life is a moving story of how he ruined his prospects and wrecked his family. But later, he became one of the leading preachers in the country at a time when people were turning to God in their thousands.

Joshua Poole grew up in a poor Yorkshire home and his intelligence won him a scholarship to Skipton Grammar School. That was in 1830—a tremendous achievement in those days! But he was a restless boy and within three years, he left school and went with his brother to live at Durham. There, they stayed with an uncle, who persuaded them to work in the mines and offered to look after their wages. They found jobs in pits where the tunnels were seldom more than 26-28 inches high and often a quarter of a mile long. They had to crawl about dragging 3 cwt. loads of coal behind them, and according to a Royal Commission investigating at the time, boys like Joss and his brother worked shifts of up to 36 hours.

The Davy Lamp had been invented twenty-five years before, but few miners used it. Candles were much brighter and meant more work and more money. Explosions and accidents were very, very common. After a long while as 'working animals', the brothers found that their uncle had swindled them by spending their money and they went home to Skipton in disgust. Joss found work and learned to play the violin. Then, when he was getting on for twenty, he decided to give up his job and make his living entertaining in the pubs. He joined up with a friend and they went on the road as travelling musicians.

Often they made a lot of money playing in pubs and fairs, but as they earned it, they drank it, and then they would walk the streets for days without food or work. Joss Poole became increasingly addicted to drinking and when he returned to his home town, he was already beyond help. He fell in love with a quiet girl named Jane and at twenty-two, he married her. She gave birth to a baby girl, but Poole treated them very badly and made no effort to support them. He usually went home drunk and when Jane became ill with tuberculosis, he was never sober to help or comfort her.

She died heartbroken and half-starved, her last effort being to knit her own burial shroud. She died in utter loneliness, her husband in bed beside her in a drunken stupor. Poole was penniless, but his father paid for Jane's funeral and said to his son, "Come to my home, only give up drinking and fiddling." Joss was cut to the heart by his conscience. And when he lost his baby daughter only a week later, he desperately wanted to be able to start life again in a new way. But his feelings passed and his good intentions went with them and within weeks of his wife's death, he made up his mind to marry his sister-in-law, Mary.

Mary was far from being keen on the idea. He was always drunk and she knew only too well how he had treated Jane. But as she saw more of him, she began to feel sorry for him, until after a while, she loved him and convinced herself that she could change him. She was a Christian girl and her principles told her that she should see the change before she married. Nevertheless, they were married after an engagement of only two months. During the first week, Poole was a model husband. Then he launched himself into his pub-life as never before. Frequently he was so drunk that he slept out in haystacks, barns and pigsties.

A serious illness brought him to his knees to pray for mercy and forgiveness from God, but as he recovered, he forgot it all and soon he returned to his favourite haunt. The landlord welcomed him and the news spread that Joss was

Home in a cellar

back with his fiddle. The house filled and celebrations commenced. It was far into the night when he returned to Mary rolling drunk. From that day, he was scarcely ever sober for seven years.

Mary gave birth to a boy, but Poole hardly knew. His old father, whose house he still lived in, decided to have a show-down with him and confronted him one night when he came in drunk. Poole reacted by attacking his father, shouting threats of murder. His sister jumped between them and Poole turned on her like an enraged beast. Neighbours, roused by the screams, rushed in and overpowered him and the following morning, his father put him out of the house. So he took Mary and their little son, rented a cellar twelve steps below street level, and called it their 'home'. It was damp, dark and dirty. Poole had little difficulty in turning it into a little hell.

He became indescribably cruel to his family and hardly ever provided for them. A second boy was born and almost the only thing which could touch Poole's heart was the sound of his children crying for food. While he played, dined and drank, his wife often begged in the street. One night, he committed such an act of violence that all his goods (such as they were) had to be pawned to pay for the damage. With the home so bare that there was only sacking for beds, his four-year-old boy became desperately ill and they knew he would die.

Years later, Poole said, "To this day, the memory of Tommy's dying moments makes me tremble. My wife ran for the doctor who said, 'There is no hope, he will shortly die'. I had begun to say there was no God, no heaven, no devil, no eternity and no punishment at all. I seized hold of Tommy and I put him on my knee. I said, 'Let me hear you say your prayers'. He put up his hands and prayed, after which he said, 'Daddy, will you go with me?' " He was moved to trembling, but when his other son died just two months later, there was still no bed in the cellar, no food and no fire. Mary buried her two sons in paupers' coffins and finally returned to the nightmare-cellar where she would never hear their voices again. There were moments of intense sorrow and tragedy,

when Poole would become sensitive to the suffering which he caused. But no human feeling or influence could prevent him from falling back into the life of sin and cruelty. Mary gave birth to two girls before the climax of horror came. Poole, as the result of his drunkenness, sustained regular delirium tremens fits. Mary had to destroy anything sharp for fear of murder, and spend nights on the pavement with a child beneath each arm. The time came when even Mary could stand it no longer and she deserted him for the 'security' of the local workhouse, numbering herself and her two girls with the unwanted and destitute. But it was no protection. Poole was enraged. He found her and claimed her with vengeance in his heart.

He attacked her—but for the last time, for he was stopped by the police, arrested, and sent for trial. The magistrates bound him over on payment of two sureties, but there wasn't anyone who would go surety for Joshua Poole, so he was committed to Wakefield Prison for six months. He was led away friendless, watched by his wife, bereft and destitute.

Poole entered the great gates at Wakefield to experiences which would never leave his memory. How well he would remember his first fit as he sat in a reception room.

"The scenes and haunts of my life rose up in the gloom of the place. Card playing, domino playing were visible in every corner. A confused crowd of strolling fiddlers and fallen girls danced and screamed round me, with all kinds of reptiles hissing and throwing out their venomous fangs and trying to coil themselves round my body and in the background, there hung the very blackness and darkness of hell."

At a quarter-to-six on his first morning, the prison bell rang and the cell door was opened. Poole was assigned to work as a cook and moved to the cooks' cells. "We slept ten in a room, the gas burned all night and the prisoners used to sit up nearly all night indulging in the most filthy conversation." Soon, Poole had his first encounter with Mr. Seth Tait, one of the prison officers. This man asked him if he had ever been to Sunday School as a child, and Poole said that he had. Then Mr. Tait began to speak to him about his wayward life, but Poole was in no mood to listen. "For the first nine weeks, I was consumed by a burning desire for revenge on Mary. I laid a plan to murder her and the children, closing with my own death at my own hand." Mr. Tait, however, did not give up. He was concerned about Poole's eternal soul and he spoke with him at every opportunity.

"From these conversations, when alone, I began to think of former days, especially the days of my boyhood. In my cell, I was nearly driven mad by the memory of my past sins, but the kindness of the officers increased. One evening, after

having made my hammock, I was pacing my cell and my eyes fell upon a Bible lying on a table. I turned to it and began reading the 51st Psalm. 'Have mercy upon me O God, according to Thy loving kindness; according to the multitude of Thy tender mercies, blot out my transgressions . . .'

"As I was reading it, my legs trembled beneath me and I shook from head to foot. The more I read, the worse I felt. I tried to kneel and pray, but it was no use. The devil came upon me and said, "It's no use; father and mother forsake you . . . wife and children have left you . . . it's no use praying.' All that day and night I felt as though my heart would break. The next morning, Mr. Tait began speaking to me and pointing me to Jesus."

Here was the man who could not be reformed by anyone or anything. But now, the power of God was at work within him and for the first time in his life, he felt the full weight of his sins and uncleanness in God's sight.

"My soul's agony for three days was almost more than I could bear. On the fourth day, Mr. Tait was writing in his office and seeing my face bathed in tears, he looked at me, saying,

'Have you not succeeded yet,
Try, try again.
Mercy's door is open set,
Try, try, again.'

"Before he had finished the verse I found peace and entered my cell that night resting by faith in Christ as my Saviour."

"All night I prayed, I sang and shouted for joy. The man in the next cell heard me singing and praying and although he had not prayed since his childhood, he prayed that night. The next day, I began telling the cooks about Jesus. Some of them laughed, others jeered, but others came to me by themselves and opened their hearts to me."

Poole wrote to his wife, who had gone to her mother's home. He told her that he had become converted and was now a believer in the Lord Jesus Christ. With breathless anxiety, he waited for a reply. It came.

"You converted! No, never. You are only acting the hypocrite to get me back and to turn me out as you did before. As for me and my children, we never intend to live with you

The fairground preacher

any more."

When the day for his release came, Poole was met by his father and went to work for him and to make his fresh start. He found a strength he had never had before to resist temptation and he joined a Wesleyan Chapel.

"Yet in my heart," he said, "there was the void of being separated from Mary whom I had so much injured and from my children. Earnestly, I prayed to God to bring about a lasting union."

Seven months after his release from Wakefield, Joss and his family were reunited and he went back to Bradford to set up a worthy home for them. His home in Bradford was opened on Sunday mornings to seventeen-year-old 'roughs' for a Bible Class. This work grew in six months to have 42 class members and was called the School for Bradford Roughs. Poole never missed an opportunity of explaining to people how he had become a Christian and how the power of God had saved him from sin, misery and self-destruction. He began to accept invitations to speak in chapels and public meetings and wherever he spoke, people crowded in to hear 'Fiddler Joss', the ex-drunkard.

By the time he was thirty-eight, he was speaking at so many meetings that he had to give up his job. His first large meetings were at Leeds where he preached to thousands of people over the course of a fortnight, and hundreds responded to the message of the Gospel as a result. But Joss Poole's main task was speaking to the lost classes of society—the alcoholics, the destitute, the tramps and the street women. He travelled the country with other evangelists and while they took the large meetings, Joss and his wife would conduct meetings in the most degraded parts of towns and cities, often in the early hours of the morning.

"Fiddler Joss"—one of the outstanding preachers of a hundred years ago, stands in the long line of souls for whom the world could do nothing at all. He destroyed himself and those nearest and dearest to him—but the love and mercy of God found him, and he prayed, 'Hide Thy face from my sins and blot out all mine iniquities.' And God heard him, forgave him, and utterly transformed him.

The House of Lords

LEADER OF THE LORDS

Viscount Alexander of Hillsborough

Earl Alexander of Hillsborough occupied a very prominent place in the political life of this country for many years. Through five years of the last war, he ruled the navy as First Lord of the Admiralty in Churchill's coalition cabinet. After the war, he became the first Minister of Defence, and finally, he spent a long period as Leader of the Opposition in the House of Lords.

Alexander was an earnest, blunt, hard working politician, noted for his determined chin and outspoken contributions to debates. "But," said the Lord Chancellor after his death, "there can be no dispute that the dominant feature of his life was his Christian faith and belief."

Albert Alexander was born in 1885 at Weston-Super-Mare. He was still a baby when his father, an engineering worker, died, leaving a wife of twenty-eight, three other children and no money. His mother went to work in a corset making business and Alexander once said, "Throughout my childhood I never remember her leaving home on a working day after a-quarter-to-eight in the morning or getting home much before half-past-nine at night, and usually she brought work home with her even then."

On his thirteenth birthday, Alexander was due to leave Barton Hill Elementary School (Weston), when his mother told him to go and enrol at the higher grade school and gave him sevenpence, which was the weekly fee. But Alexander could not bring himself to stay on at school with money so short and he found himself a job as an office boy in a leather firm. Instead of school, he went to evening classes, and before long, changed to a better job with the Bristol School Board.

At twenty, Alexander began to think very seriously about

his relationship to God. He had been brought up to believe in God, and he attended church (playing for the church football team)—but his belief did not really mean anything to him. It was outward religion. Then he found himself attending a Baptist Church in Weston-Super-Mare and listening to the preaching of the Rev. J. T. Dawson. It was there, following a talk with the minister in his vestry, that Alexander first believed in the Lord Jesus Christ as the only One through whom sins can be forgiven. Mr. Dawson wrote to him in the First World War saying, "You know how I cherish you for that Sunday evening in my vestry long ago! I love every memory of your usefulness since. May you win through to the crown of life."

Alexander recalled this experience in the House of Lords, when he told the peers: "I was brought up in the Church of England and was in it until the age of twenty-two. Indeed, I should have been in it now if I had not discovered a bigger and wider truth. That is: that you cannot live on family, traditional religion. If you want salvation, you need to be born again. You have to go to the life-giving Word of God: the Word made flesh."

Soon after, Alexander married and together, the young couple sought to serve Christ in their lives. Although he had a nervous stammer, he was persuaded to speak at mid-week Bible Study meetings at his church, and eventually, he went out lay-preaching. He completely overcame his speaking difficulty and took on the work of lay pastor at a small chapel outside Weston-Super-Mare.

By now, he was working for the Somerset County Council as Clerk to the Education Committee. He studied in his spare time and gained slow but steady promotion at work. But at this point, his lifelong aim began to waver and he began to form ideas about life and people which were to master him for many years.

Alexander began to admire the strenuous social activities of the Co-operative movement. He saw that this movement had a tremendous potential for putting right social evils. And although he was a fervent and sincere preacher of the need of conversion for every sinner, he came to think that the main purpose of Christianity was simply to make the world a better place to live in. He began to see the Church, not as a mission to the souls of men, but as a super-social-welfare-service.

Wilberforce committed himself to social reform, but he never lost sight of the fact that Christianity was following Christ. He was always anxious and ready to rescue the souls of men and to persuade them that they needed to be saved. He always remembered that this is a doomed world and while he sought to help men socially, he knew that their greatest need was to know God. But the young Alexander was no Wilberforce. When he committed himself to social reform, his Saviour became squeezed out of his life.

After the First World War (during which Alexander had risen from private to captain), he took a job as a full-time trade union officer in Somerset, where he spent two years negotiating better working conditions for local government officers. Then, through his schoolgirl daughter, Alexander had the opportunity of a lifetime. His daughter was due to take a scholarship and the day before the examination, he said to her, "If you win this scholarship, I tell you what we'll do . . . we'll all go up to London for a fortnight's holiday to celebrate."

She passed—and the family went to London. While there, Alexander heard that the Co-operative Society was looking for a Parliamentary Secretary. It was a considerable step forward and would mean a move to London. He applied and was at length selected for the post from a very large number of well qualified applicants. At first, he did not find enough work to do. But the day came when Sir Thomas Allen, Chairman of the Co-operative Congress, walked into the office and said, "Here's a job for you. I want you to defeat the Lloyd-George government." A new method of taxing company profits was passing through Parliament and it threatened to eat into Co-op dividends. Alexander got to work persuading M.P.s, touring the country for meetings, and mounting as effective a campaign as he could, to preserve the 'rights' of the Co-op. And he won. Against seemingly impossible odds, he killed the offending proposals. Sir Thomas Allen looked at him with raised eyebrows. He had hardly expected success. "Young man," he said, "you had better go into Parliament." Sir Thomas pronounced—and it was done.

In 1922, Albert Alexander stood as Co-operative candidate for the Hillsborough constituency of Sheffield and was elected to Parliament.

He was now living in Twickenham and was very keen on attending a church where the 'social gospel' was preached. The teaching was that everyone should live in brotherly kindness towards their fellowmen and the world would gradually become a better place until the Kingdom of God was ushered in. The teaching of the Bible had been mainly placed on one side, and preachers were substituting ideas of their own which they imagined were better. Alexander was now fully convinced that his duty was to improve the conditions of men by social welfare and political legislation. A better world would make a better people. He said so in pulpits on Sundays (he still did some lay preaching). He said so in Co-operative public meetings, usually held on Sundays. He said so in articles which he wrote for the Brotherhood Movement.

Many people in Parliament regarded Alexander as no more than a 'Co-op' representative. It was probably to keep the Co-operative movement happy that he was made First Lord of the Admiralty in the 1929 Labour Government. Whatever the motives behind his appointment, he has been described as one of the outstanding successes of that particular Cabinet. Suddenly everyone realised his ability. But after two years, he lost his office and his Parliamentary seat in the landslide defeat of the Government in 1931. He had to wait four years before he could return, then he gradually moved towards greater honours.

In the early stages of the last war, Churchill left his post as First Lord of the Admiralty to take over the helm as Prime Minister. The navy had been Churchill's chief interest and it weighed very heavily upon him to appoint a strong and capable man to succeed him at the Admiralty. Without hesitation and with complete confidence, Churchill appointed A. V. Alexander, who remained First Lord to the end of the war. In many ways, the war was a cruel blow to Alexander's confused philosophy of life. The ugliness of war showed up the fallen nature of man. It showed him to be too far gone for reformation by education, prosperity and good govern-

King George VI with Alexander outside the Admiralty

ment. Daily, individual men and women were facing problems
of life and death. A relationship with God was the burning
need of millions of people—and their social and bodily needs
paled into insignificance besides.

One of Alexander's responsibilities at the Admiralty was to
appoint a new Astronomer Royal. He selected his man—a
Cambridge professor—and sent for him. He offered him the
appointment, but the professor asked for a week in which to
think it over. When Alexander saw him again, he declined the
highest honour of his profession, because he felt he must

continue to devote his leisure time to Christian work among university students. Alexander was deeply moved. He left the Admiralty that day and went home greatly affected. This man had room in his life for the SOULS of men. As for Alexander —he had left that behind in his earliest days as a lay-preacher.

Gradually he found his way back to the teaching of the Bible. He had never ceased to believe in the Lord Jesus, whom he had given his life to at the age of twenty-two. But he had put the ideas of 'religious' men before the teaching of God's Word and had missed the closeness of a walk with God, which is God's purpose for all His children. He never left off working to improve the living conditions of men. But he came back to the point where he said that the only answer for the human soul was the sacrificial death of Christ.

How would the Kingdom of God come? His sixty years of Socialism had taught him that it would not come by politics and he said so (a few years later) in speaking to large audiences.

After the war, Alexander became the first Minister of Defence—a new office, coming under heavy fire at one point for a double change of mind about whether National Service should be 12 months or 18 months. Then, after five years on defence, he was created a viscount (1950) and went to the Lords. He bought a 220 acre farm at West Mersea and used to travel up to the House of Lords every day from there.

In 1955, Alexander, aged seventy, was unanimously elected Leader of the Opposition in the Lords. His activity was amazing for a man of his years. Firstly, there was a full programme of affairs to lead in the Lords. Then he would often be found on the platform of large public meetings (especially Protestant meetings). He opened churches, spoke at office Christian Union meetings, and sometimes preached on Sundays.

The Rev. William Hancock, of West Mersea Union Church, spoke of his membership of the local church. "It was our privilege here to know Lord Alexander as a Christian man. He and her ladyship became members of our church in June 1956 and I think it is true to say that Lord Alexander loved this little place of worship. We shall sorely miss him; for his membership was expressed in practical terms, and every

Sunday morning, if he was in residence on the Island, would see him in his place in church, whatever the weather, and toward the end, however ill he was feeling. I said to him once, 'My Lord, you are an example to men half your age,' 'Ah!' he replied, 'You see, Hancock, I have been forgiven so much.' "

On May 10th 1961, Christian unity was debated in the Lords. While other peers expressed the view that having one, united church with no doctrinal basis, was the most important aim for the day, Lord Alexander made it quite clear that a man's belief decided whether or not he was a real Christian.

"If you look at the fifth chapter of John's Gospel, verse 39, you find that the Master says, 'Search the Scriptures: for in them ye think ye have eternal life.' There is no other place to search for eternal life but here. Jesus never said, 'What saith the Sanhedrim, or the high priests, or the archbishops or bishops, or the Pope,' but 'What saith the Scriptures'."

Alexander firmly believed that the bulk of the professing Church could not really be classified as 'Christian' at all, because it had not taken its religion from Christ and the Scriptures.

"I believe," he said in the Lords, "that you can find salvation for man only through the Word of Life and what it says in the Bible—I take you to the way of salvation . . . 'I am the way, the truth, and the life: no man cometh unto the Father, but by Me'."

What greater tribute could be paid to the latter life of Lord Alexander, than that spoken by an Earl who did not share his spiritual convictions. Lord Longford said, "He based his life on the Bible. He knew it through and through, as no other layman in the House could perhaps claim to know it. Daily he strove, by prayer and scrutiny of conscience, to carry out the will of God as he understood it. He pursued that end as ardently in his last years as I imagined in the days when he was a young preacher—perhaps even more so . . . he pursued it with a conviction, a candour and commitment that were the visible source of his strength . . ."

Earl Alexander of Hillsborough died in January 1965.

c

SAILOR, DESERTER, SLAVE-TRADER

John Newton

John Newton was the only son of a sea captain who owned a small fleet of private trading vessels. Old Captain Newton planned a rugged upbringing for John. He would go to school not a day longer than was necessary, then he would go to sea, visiting ports and meeting people of all nationalities—the best education a boy could have. John's mother had died when he was seven, but in those early years she had stored his mind with Bible teaching. After her death, he was sent to boarding school until he was eleven, when his father's plan came into operation.

John was taken away from school and given his first taste of months at sea and exciting days in Mediterranean ports. He entered into the life with relish and soon picked up the ways and language of the seamen. He went to extremes in his behaviour and when the voyage was over, he felt sickened and ashamed of himself. But these thoughts were soon brushed aside and after a while on dry land, John became bored, moody and frustrated.

His father found space for him on another ship and he was occupied again. Voyage followed voyage and on each one, his conduct at sea became more abandoned and his conscience more hardened. Once, when he was home, John arranged to meet some friends to look over a warship anchored in the harbour. He arrived at the quayside too late to meet his friends and saw them in the boat which was taking visitors to the warship. Suddenly his disappointment was turned into horror as the boat capsized, drowning his friends. The tragedy haunted him, the reality of death came home to him, and he felt terrified of having to meet God himself with a guilty conscience. In later years he wrote, "I often saw religion as a means of escaping Hell, but I loved sin and was unwilling to leave it."

Captain Newton saw that his son had become even more moody than ever and arranged for him to go on an unusually long voyage. Before going, John was given three days to carry out some business for his father in Deal, Kent. In the house where he lodged, he met Mary Catlett, a girl who immediately became the idol of his life. The three days became three weeks and John returned home to face the rage of his father for having missed his ship. What was to be done with the boy now? Captain Newton's only answer was another voyage. But to the lovesick John, the voyage seemed to last for years and as soon as he returned, he made straight for Mary. Again he frustrated the plans of his father by overstaying his visit. Captain Newton lost his patience—he even thought of disowning John. Then, out of the blue came a stunning shock for John, but a shock which Captain Newton secretly welcomed.

Young Newton was roaming the streets wearing his seaman's check shirt when he was spotted by a lieutenant of the Royal Navy. The navy needed strong blooded youths to fight the French fleet and young Newton became one of those who were ruthlessly press-ganged aboard H.M.S. Harwich. On hearing the news, old Captain Newton made no effort to claim his son, but calmly sent a note to the captain of the Harwich recommending him for a midshipman's post. This rank gave Newton certain privileges, but he resented his enlistment and despised his appointment.

The Harwich set sail and took up station in the English Channel waiting for the rest of the fleet to assemble. Newton was given a day's leave ashore. He spent three days with Mary at Deal and returned to suffer the discipline of the Royal Navy. The fleet left Spithead in January 1745 and immediately ran into a freak sou' westerly gale. Many ships were driven onto the Cornish coast, while others, including the Harwich, fled for the shelter of Plymouth harbour. Newton heard that his father was in Torbay—about twenty miles away. If only they could speak together, he was sure that he could persuade his father to give him a permanent position in his Mediterranean trading fleet. Newton had been warned once against desertion, but how else could he reach his father? The opportunity came when he was put in charge of a landing party with special orders to watch out for possible deserters. He made a break for it himself and followed the road to Torbay. All went well until he was just outside Torbay. He was then stopped and questioned by a group of soldiers who clapped him in irons and marched him back to Plymouth.

On board H.M.S. Harwich, a humiliating punishment awaited him. A gathering of the whole ship's company was called and in front of them all, Newton was stripped, whipped, degraded to the lowest rank, and his midshipmen friends officially forbidden to speak to him.

Newton became indescribably depressed. His back was cut to ribbons, he had no friends to speak to and he was employed on the most menial jobs aboard ship. Worst of all, he had little or no hope of ever seeing Mary again, for the fleet was leaving Plymouth for five years' service in the East Indies. There was nothing left to live for, and in his heart Newton blamed God for his predicament. Living in the company of the more abandoned, godless sailors, Newton adapted himself to suit their ways. He won their approval by acting the young tearaway, and he not only listened to filthy and blasphemous jokes, but to their admiration, made up new and better ones. He lived for the pleasure of being respected as the instigator of everything godless.

After some time, the fleet called in at Madeira for stores. On the last night of their stay, Newton was sleeping when his hammock was suddenly cut from its ropes. A voice hissed in his ear, "If you can pack your bags in five minutes, you'll see the last of the Harwich." Without question Newton obeyed. A midshipman who felt sorry for him had got him on deck to be the first volunteer for a surprise vacancy which was going on another boat. Now he had the opportunity for a new start. But he threw it away. On the new ship, he deliberately set out to mock God and to be the ringleader of everything foul.

There was a civilian passenger on the new ship who was a slave trader and who was returning to Sierra Leone where negroes were captured. His name was Clow and it was obvious that slave trading paid him very well. Newton hatched a scheme to cultivate a friendship with Clow, and to try to get

a discharge from the navy at Sierra Leone so that he could
join Clow's activities. The discharge was granted on condition
that Newton forfeited all his back pay. When the time came,
he went ashore—a penniless recruit to the slave trade.

No sooner had he set foot on dry land than Newton went
down with malaria. Clow couldn't have cared less. He set off
on an expedition, leaving Newton in the hands of his negro
mistress who so hated the new Englishman, that she took steps
to prevent him from recovering. She gave him a plank for a
bed and a log for a pillow. Delirious and unable to move, he
was left out in the torturing sun to die. But the woman had
underestimated his strength and after a few weeks, he began to
show signs of recovery. Half starved and semi-conscious, he
attempted to walk. Meetings of slaves were organised to jeer
at him and mimic his crazy, staggering movements.

He was given no food and had to go to the plantation at
the dead of night and unearth the raw, root vegetables to
keep alive. Somehow he recovered from the fever, and as
soon as the opportunity came, he dashed off S.O.S. letters
from the settlement to his father.

When Clow returned, Newton complained bitterly about
his treatment, but Clow resented his complaints. The two set
out in a boat to find slaves further down the coast. When
another companion falsely accused Newton of stealing,
Clow's resentment found its outlet. He had Newton chained
to the blistering deck of the boat and victimised for several
months. Then, a passing trader asked Clow if he had any
spare helpers and Newton was transferred. Soon, Newton
found his way to a settlement where a wealthy plantation
owner gave him a job. Back in England, Captain Newton had
received his son's S.O.S. letter and had arranged for a trading
ship named 'The Greyhound' to call at Clow's settlement
and collect him. Help was on the way. The Greyhound had a
crew of about thirty and traded at most of the settlements
along the West African coast. But when they called for
Newton, they were told that he had moved away long ago.
Then, when they were about a hundred miles down the
coast, the ship's watch reported a smoke signal from the
shore. This usually indicated that trading was invited, so The
Greyhound put ashore and found Newton cooking a meal

The way of life aboard a large man-o-war.

over a fire.

He was welcomed aboard as a passenger and gentleman and settled down to a life of ease. At twenty three years of age, his fortunes had turned. But with nothing to do, he channelled his behaviour and thinking even further into a terrible vortex of sin. He would 'preach' from the ship's Bible, twisting the text into the most vile stories. Even hardened sailors began to find his 'jokes' sickening and the ship's captain disliked him intensely. He regarded Newton as a Jonah and believed something disastrous would happen to the ship because of him. And it did. As soon as they finished their trading, they

put out to open sea to return home. At midnight, the calm
water suddenly burst into raging seas and the ship was struck
by a tropical typhoon. Newton awoke to find the cabin full
of water and the ship pitching and rolling violently. He
climbed to the top deck to find mountainous waves crashing
across the deck. "I'll man the pumps," shouted Newton.
"No," yelled the captain, "fetch me a knife from below."
Turning to obey, Newton saw a man at the pumps swept
overboard by another gigantic wave. If he had gone to the
pumps, he would have been lost.

One side of the ship was almost completely battered to
pieces and water was pouring in so fast that it couldn't be
pumped out. It was amazing that the ship remained afloat.
The sailors were demoralised and convinced that the end had
come, while the captain was cursing Newton, the Jonah, for
ever having come aboard. It was only then that Newton,
lashed to the deck for safety and working the pumps, began
to realise the staggering truth of the situation. It was surely
impossible for The Greyhound to ride any more of these
colossal waves. The colour drained from his face and his
mocking, arrogant jokes gave way to fear and serious thought.
"Is there a God?" he began to ask himself. "Is there a life
after death?" The very thought of death seemed to confirm
that there was. His instincts warned him to prepare himself
to meet his Maker, the very thing which frightened him most.
How could he face the One Whom he had insulted all his life?
He began to feel a crushing despair.

He turned to look at the area of the ship which he had
been pumping. "If that won't do," he said, "the Lord have
mercy upon us." Suddenly, for the first time in years, his
blasphemous words seemed to bite back at him. "What mercy
do I deserve?" he thought. The answer was painfully obvious.

He was moved from the pumps to take a turn wrestling
with the helm and as he did so, his thoughts raced feverishly
over all that he knew about God.

"I now began to think of that Lord Jesus whom I had so
often ridiculed. I remembered the details of His life and
death, a death for the punishment of sins not His own, but
for the sake of all those who should put their trust in Him.
How could I trust Him to bear my punishment? I really

A typical scene in the Midshipmen's Mess.

wanted proof that God could do this. I wished that these things were true."

Expecting to die at any moment, Newton prayed desperately to God for help and safety. The answer to his frantic prayers was to come more quickly than he could have expected. As daylight came, the fury of the storm diminished and the back-breaking work of operating the pumps seemed to be having some effect. The damaged side was hastily patched up with planks and sealed with blankets. Then it was Newton's turn for some rest. But how could he rest? Seizing a Bible, he went into his cabin and read these words:—

"Jesus said to them, ask and you will find, knock and it will be opened to you, for every asker receives, and every seeker finds and to everyone who knocks, the door will be opened. What father among you whose son asks for bread, will give him a stone? If you then, evil minded as you are, know enough to give good gifts to your children, how much more shall the Heavenly Father give the Holy Spirit to those who ask Him?"

Under threat of death, Newton had thought more clearly than ever before. "Upon this I reasoned—if the Bible is true as a whole, then this particular passage must be true. The writer, if he is God, has promised to give the Spirit to all who ask for it. Therefore I must ask for it. And if I am given it, then I must trust the whole Bible as God's Word."

With his mind grappling with spiritual problems, one other thing worried him. He could see that God could forgive some people their sins. In everyday life, one can forgive a friend for some trifling offence. But to forgive your arch-enemy is impossible. Why should he expect God to do this? The answer lay in the Bible. He read about Saul, the man who had hated Christ and persecuted Christians. Saul had been forgiven and re-named the apostle Paul. So, perhaps there could be mercy for him too.

The furious typhoon had given way to a gentle breeze. But it had left them with a helpless, unseaworthy ship, no knowledge of their position, and most of the supplies washed overboard. Every man aboard knew that the slightest change in the wind would be enough to send them all to the bottom. A rough course was set and they prepared for the perilous journey back to England.

Day after day, the men manned the pumps to keep down the water which was constantly seeping into the damaged hull. They tried to satisfy their hunger on tiny sections of salted cod and they began to feel the effects of exposure and semi-starvation. As the days passed, they grew too weak to man the pumps and one seaman died. The food ran out and then the water, and everything seemed lost at last. But that very day, the battered Greyhound sighted a small island off Lough Swilley, Northern Ireland, and they landed, knowing they had survived the impossible.

"About that time," wrote Newton, "I began to know that there is a God who hears and answers prayer. I felt a peace and satisfaction on that day which I had never known before."

This experience made such a difference to John Newton that his life became wholly changed. Although he continued to work on slave ships for a time (becoming captain of the 'Duke of Argyle') he later came to be one of the most earnest opponents of slavery. He married Mary Catlett and longed to devote himself to the Lord who had forgiven him and granted him a new life. For some years he held the post of Tide Surveyor at Liverpool, and served as lay pastor in a nearby independent church. Then he was appointed curate of Olney Parish Church in Bedfordshire. Newton drew large numbers of people to his preaching, started one of the first Sunday schools in the country and wrote some of the finest and best known hymns. Together with the poet William Cowper, who also lived at Olney, he compiled a hymn book from which scores of hymns were taken which are still used today.

After sixteen years at Olney, Newton was called to London where he ministered until his death. He was certainly one of the greatest men of his day. Men such as William Wilberforce could point to Newton as an instrument of God in their spiritual lives.

No biography of Newton can afford to leave out the words which he ordered to be used on his own gravestone:-

Once an infidel and libertine, a servant of slaves in Africa was by the rich mercy of our Lord and Saviour Jesus Christ preserved, restored, pardoned and appointed to preach the faith he had long laboured to destroy.

THE MAN BEHIND THE RED CROSS

Jean Henri Dunant

The life story of Henri Dunant is without doubt one of the most extraordinary that can be found. It is the story of a man who was at the same time one of the greatest failures and one of the greatest successes of recent history. It is the story of a man who dined with kings, and ate crusts with tramps. The story of a hard-headed and self-seeking man of the world, who had more conscience and feeling than any other public figure of his time.

The fast moving adventure of this man's seemingly contradictory life spanned the glamour and gore of a changing Europe, from 1828 to 1910. Dunant spent his boyhood amidst the sumptuous surroundings of wealthy Geneva, in Switzerland. His family were rich, his father being a landowning city councillor. Both his parents were devout churchgoers and Dunant, a broad shouldered, red-headed, seventeen-year-old was soon searching out the answers to spiritual questions for himself. What was a Christian? How could a man know God? What was the purpose of life? A dynamic teacher and preacher had burst upon Geneva like a fireball. He was Pastor Louis Gaussen, who preached Sunday after Sunday in Geneva's largest church—packed to the doors. There, in the crowded pews, young Henri Dunant listened regularly to the preaching of the Gospel and became deeply affected. By the time he was eighteen, he was a praying Christian whose life and future was surrendered to Christ. He lost no time in finding ways of spreading his new-found faith to others. Every Sunday at two o'clock, he passed through the grim, iron doors of the City prison to visit prisoners in their cells. For his student friends, he organised weekly rambles over the hills, the main topic of conversation being—the Gospel. Before very long,

77

these rambles were attracting over a hundred young people.
Always they were rounded off by a meeting held in Dunant's
house, where, amidst the white pillars and dark panelling of
his father's great reception hall, many of his friends found
the way to God.

This meeting grew into the first Y.M.C.A. in Switzerland,
and the parent of many others, for as members moved away
to work or study in other parts of Europe, they started
similar meetings for young people. Dunant himself, who
became a travelling bank executive, kept in touch with all
these offshoots, and held them together. So full of drive was
he as organiser of these many meetings, that a fellow worker
wrote, "My task has not been an easy one. I had Dunant to
restrain—he has amazing zeal and energy.

"It was he who knew how to knot the threads that broke,
to rally the backsliders, stimulate those who weakened and
warm the fainthearted." As a young Christian, Dunant had
virtually become the founder and mainspring of the European
Y.M.C.A.

His organising and diplomatic skill was also noticed by
those in his profession, and at twenty-six, after representing
his bank successfully in North Africa, he was made general
manager of all its investments in Algeria. So, as the head of a
big business, Dunant found himself in a new and challenging
country—once run by fanatical tribesmen, but now brought
into subjection by French valour. His task was to organise the
development of mines, factories, homes and farms in estates
covering 50,000 acres.

Dunant's life had been spent among wealth, but the wealth
of Geneva did not pamper its owners. Personal spending was
always restricted and self indulgence or extravagance frowned
upon on principle. In French conquered Algeria, wealth
meant luxury, status, power and vast possessions. A war
broke out in Dunant's mind as he dreamed of Oriental
wealth, and at the same time tried to honour his Lord and
live for Him. He continued to visit his European Y.M.C.A.
meetings and to live more or less as an obedient Christian.
He thought that there would be no harm in indulging his
ambitions for more wealth and success to just a small degree.
Although it was in breach of his conditions of employment,

Nineteenth century Geneva.

Dunant tried a little speculative business of his own, buying land and selling it at a profit. Then he went further and secured a lease of over a thousand acres of ground from the government to develop plantation, mining and factory interests. His 'small step' cost him his job as general manager for the Genevan banking company and he was plunged headlong into seeking his fortune as a private speculator in Algeria. Slowly, he became consumed by his ambition and desire for success and wealth and his heart grew cold towards God. His memories of youth faded into the background and his entire energy was devoted to building his empire.

While a banking executive, Dunant had moved in very high circles and he knew many rich and influential people—like General de Beaufort, the Chief of Staff of Napoleon III. From his many contacts, he now secured many thousands of francs

by way of investments for the development of his Algerian
estates—investments on which he had to pay a 10 per cent
annual return. He constructed the most modern mills, built
homes and laid out plantations, anticipating that he would
soon get planning permission for access to water supplies.
But all Dunant's diplomacy, banking skill and contacts in the
French Government could not hurry the French Algerian
authorities into granting the water rights he so desperately
needed. Without water, the estates did not earn a penny, but
investors still had to be paid interest.

After a year of frustration and delay, Dunant was in a
panic. He had tried almost everything—there was only one
thing left for him to do. He would petition the Emperor,
Napoleon III of France.

At that time, Napoleon had decided to help Italy regain her
full territory, which was largely occupied by the Austrians.
The French and Italian allies began the first 'modern' war—
in which railroads and telegraphs were used, and war corres-
pondents sent their dramatic despatches back to their papers.
It started on Italian soil with the French gaining rapid victories
over Austrian forces. Dunant made up his mind to get an
audience with Napoleon III while he was commanding his
troops in Italy. He might be there for months, and time was
short for Dunant.

He intended to interest the French Emperor in a book he
had written about him. It was a book crammed with flattery
for Napoleon's international achievements and aims. Then he
hoped to show how his own Algerian estates were wasting
away because of local government indolence in granting
planning permission for water. Dunant got to the front line
and found his friend General de Beaufort, who told him how
to get to Napoleon's H.Q. A great encounter was about to
take place at Solferino (near Brescia) and Napoleon had with
him 150,000 men with 400 cannon.

Secure in the hills were the troops of Emperor Francis
Joseph of Austria. There were 170,000 of them, with 500 cannon occupying the fortified heights of Solferino. Altogether,
over 300,000 men were facing each other along a ten mile
front. Dunant arrived on the fringe of it all by daybreak on
24th June 1859. At 6 a.m., Austrian foot soldiers, who had

not eaten, began to advance towards the French line. Hordes of white coated men followed, their giant standards bearing the Imperial Eagle. Bugles and drums sounded, and the massive French line also began to move, the armour of Lancers and Dragoons catching the early sun.

To Dunant, it seemed to start like a game—puffs of white smoke—crackling of muskets—and thousands of colourful uniforms. But suddenly, it developed into the most terrible butchery, as men charged each other with bayonets, fought with stones and knives, and fell by the hundred as musket and cannon fire swept down from the hills. When the foot soldiers were in deadlock, the cavalry galloped over the strewn bodies, followed by the gun carriages, killing and crushing countless wounded men. Wave after wave of Frenchmen attempted to storm the fortified hills held by the Austrians, until a fearful thunderstorm broke, and under a cloudburst, they swarmed through the cordon of cannon and into the town of Solferino.

The Austrian line was broken and the retreat began. Even Napoleon was stunned and appalled at the enormous cost of his victory as he sat on his white stallion, chain smoking. From the fringe of it all, Dunant was living out a nightmare. He wrote:

"When the sun rose on the twenty-fifth, it disclosed the most dreadful sights imaginable. Bodies of men and horses covered the battlefield; corpses were strewn over roads, ditches, ravines, thickets and fields; the approaches of Solferino were literally thick with dead. It took three days and three nights to bury the dead on the battlefield . . . the bodies were piled by the hundred in great common graves.

The wounded on the battlefield lay their heads in muddy, bloodstained puddles to drink—at least forty thousand of them, young men with all visions of victory and glory shattered. Dunant made his way to nearby Castiglione, expecting to find Napoleon's H.Q. Instead, he found hundreds of gravely wounded soldiers of both armies piled in churches and on the pavements. Napoleon had moved on. There was food, water and lint available, but the peasants were panic stricken and there were no doctors to attend to anything. So, for three days and three nights, Dunant lived out the nightmare

he was to remember all his life, as he organised and led the
medical relief work among the dead and dying of the Battle
of Solferino.

He was called 'the man in white' and almost revered as
an angel. With a few peasants and helpers, he fed the men and
dressed their wounds, until a handful of doctors arrived to
begin some field operations.

On the fourth day, he found a cart and set off to locate the
Emperor. He had to save his Algerian business empire, and to
do that, he had to see Napoleon. Napoleon could not be
seen. Neither were his aides in the least helpful. But Dunant
hardly cared. He was torn in two by the experience of
Solferino and his three days with the thousands of wounded
men. He came out of it all like a man who had been brain-
washed and nothing—not even his mounting business worries
—could get Solferino out of his mind.

Eventually, he sat down and poured his memories out on
paper to produce a book which shocked the world and moved
heads of state. It was 'Souvenir de Solferino', in which he
recounted in detail the horrors of the battle and its aftermath
and in which he called for relief societies whose aim would be
to provide care for the wounded while being recognised as
neutral by both sides on the battlefield. Immediate practical
support for Dunant's idea came from a group of prominent
men in his native Geneva, and a retired general, a distinguished
lawyer and two doctors joined him to form the famous
Committee of Five.

They decided to hold a conference and invited heads of
government to send representatives. Dunant, meanwhile, went
to a Berlin conference to get support for his scheme. In
Berlin, the idea of neutral relief workers mushroomed out to
include neutral recognition for all the injured also. Dunant
was given an audience by the King of Saxony and won the
approval of almost everyone. Then he went to Austria, and
on to Geneva, where the first international conference was
soon to begin. The salesmanship and diplomacy of Dunant
had carried sixteen governments, of which fourteen (including
Britain) sent delegates.

But all the time Dunant travelled round Europe promoting
the Red Cross, his troubles in Algeria loomed larger and

larger. Once again, Dunant pinned everything on his hero—
Napoleon III. If only he could get an audience. Napoleon was
due to make a state visit to Algeria and Dunant made sure he
was officially invited to be presented to him. The great day
came when Dunant, who had ready access to the sovereigns
of Europe, at last stood before the elusive French Emperor.
He told him about the Red Cross, and then he told him about
his business problems due to the absence of water on his
estates. The Emperor promised to help, and Dunant went his
way as if walking on air. Full of optimism, he went in for

further investments and developments. Napoleon, however, did nothing at all to help him.

Then came plague and war in Algeria, followed by cholera, locusts, earthquakes, drought and the most terrible winter ever recorded. Dunant's estates were tottering on the very brink of ruin. The business empire which he had abandoned God for was about to collapse. He shut his eyes in blind hope and turned back to pre-occupy himself with the Red Cross. It was soon to be tested as an organisation.

In Prussia, the notorious Bismark had cast his sinister shadow across the international scene. Dominating the King, he forced a terrible and unnecessary war with Austria in which two armies of a quarter-of-a-million men clashed. The Prussians were equipped with the new breech loading rifles, with which they crushed the Austrian troops. 25,000 men died. The Geneva Convention was observed for the first time, but while Prussian Red Cross teams cleared all their wounded, the Austrians had no Red Cross organisation and their wounded men lay in the open throughout two days and nights of heavy rain, until Prussian relief workers found them. It was both a triumph for the Red Cross, and a bitter indictment of governments which refused to make provision for their wounded.

Dunant was honoured in a banquet thrown by the Berlin Royal Household. But they did not know that Dunant's financial collapse was about to take place. His biggest bank overdraft was called in. Investors asked for their money back. Everything had to go—his property, mills, oak forests, lead and gold mines, and his family fortune. In Geneva, nothing was more disgraceful than bankruptcy, so that poor Dunant, living in Paris, dare not go home. His fellow leaders of the International Red Cross were embarrassed by him and cut him off, depriving him of his office.

Up till now, life for Dunant had amounted to flights of brilliance—when his genius for planning and unsurpassed diplomacy forged history. But at the same time, life always seemed to hold him on the edge of a precipice of doom and destruction. In the midst of success he was in failure. The fears and shadows of business collapse spread round everything. After his financial ruin, there were fewer and fewer opportunities for brilliance. His rich education and a small income kept him respectable for a time and international flare-ups summoned him out of oblivion to organise Red Cross activities.

During the great war between France and Prussia when Bismark humiliated and routed Napoleon III, Dunant made a dramatic under-cover escape from Paris while it was under seige, in order to begin diplomatic discussions with the Germans. But apart from such brief moments of 'glory', Dunant was a spent out man. At one point, he came to England and was glad to take a job trying to sell a gas operated organ invention. Back in Paris, only in his early fifties, he was forced to join the ranks of the poor. He had no money and frequently could not even pay for a night's lodging. He spent long, dreary days trudging round the cold Paris streets, with no relatives or friends—haunted by his memories and his pathetic failure. Jean Henri Dunant had disappeared from public life. He had abandoned his Lord for status and riches; placed his trust in his brains and his business; depended upon the Emperor, and looked to a vain world to keep its material-istic promises. But like Lot of old in the City of Sodom—it had come to nothing and he had lost his peace.

Lost by the world and shunned by his friends, Dunant's hopes turned to a Friend who had once said, "I will never leave you, nor forsake you." Far away from the scenes of earthly disgrace and failure, he went back to Jesus, laid his sins and his past at the Cross of Calvary, and found once again the reality of walking with God and knowing Him. The prodigal had returned.

Dunant was an old man when he was rediscovered by the world. Suddenly the schoolmaster of a small town in the Swiss Alps realised that the lovable 'patriarch' with the long white beard, living in the pensioner's hospital, was the long lost founder of the Red Cross. A Swiss journalist came to investigate—and the story was headline news round the world. Immediately, there was great acclamation, culminating in the award to Dunant of the first Nobel Prize. His rediscovery and his prize meant a great deal to him. But it was nothing by comparison to his rediscovery of Christ and the prize of knowing Him.

Martin Luther nails up his Ninety-five Theses

DAWN BREAKS OVER EUROPE

Martin Luther

Martin Luther grew up amidst the peasants and poverty of a small mining town in fifteenth-century Germany. His father was a woodcutter who later became the manager of a small foundry, smelting iron. He was a hardworking man, but a formidable father, ruling his sons with a rod of iron.

In those days, school was a place where knowledge was driven into boys by fear of punishment. It was closely bound up with the Catholic Church and young Martin Luther was well and truly indoctrinated with the fear of God and the power of the Pope. He once said that whenever he heard the name of Christ as a child, he turned pale with fright because he imagined a terrible judge who would one day dominate eternity.

Martin was fourteen when he went away to 'high school', but as there was not enough money to keep him, he had to join the ranks of the poor students begging a living in the streets, until one day, a wealthy family took pity on him and gave him the hospitality of their home. Luther was such an exceptional student, that he was urged to go on with his studies. So, at the age of eighteen, he set off for the most famous place of learning in Germany—the University of Erfurt. As his father had become financially better off, Luther could afford to take a room and support himself at Erfurt and he studied so hard that by the age of twenty-two, he passed the examinations to be a master of arts and a doctor of philosophy.

But his academic triumphs could not suppress a fear which had come to worry him. "What about my soul?" he thought. "Where is God and what takes place in eternity?" And when one of his closest friends was murdered, the thought came back with greater force. "What would happen to me if I were suddenly called away without warning?"

Young Doctor Luther soon took up the status and privileges of a lecturer at the University. His parents were very proud of him and showed it when he went home to spend his first holiday with them as a 'doctor'. They had no idea that their pride and happiness was about to be shattered and their son's career thrown away—all in the panic of a few moments. It happened while Luther was walking the last stage of his return journey to Erfurt. Quite suddenly, he was caught in a tremendous thunderstorm. The rain poured down, but Luther moved slowly on; then a blinding roll of lightning seared through the sky and struck the ground ahead of him.

He fell, certain that his end had come. Terrified, he shouted, "Help! Beloved Anne help, and I will immediately become a monk." The peal of thunder passed away and Luther, still shaking, rose to his feet. He was stunned, surprised to be alive, and more agitated than ever before about his standing in the sight of his Maker. He felt there was no other course open to him than to keep his vow and to enter the monastery. He was about to submit himself to be bound by the very chains of superstition and man-made religion which years later he was to shatter, ushering in the Reformation of Europe.

It was a very pale and shaken Luther who returned to Erfurt. He invited all his friends to a final supper-party at his room and broke the news that he was going into a monastery. They all pleaded with him to change his mind, but nothing would persuade him. When the party was cleared away and all his friends had gone, Luther set out—at the dead of night—to apply for admission to St. Augustine's Monastery.

"I thought God was not concerned about me and if I got to heaven, it would depend mostly upon me. I knew no better than to think that by my own accomplishments, I must rid myself of sin ... so I became a monk and came in for a most bitter experience at the same time. Oh, I thought that if I went into the monastery cloisters to serve God in a cowl, with head shorn, He would reward me and bid me welcome." So Dr. Martin Luther, aged twenty-two, bid goodbye to the world, returned his degree gown to the University, and wrote

to inform his horrified father.

His first lesson from the monastery was intended to make him humble. He was given cleaning, fetching and carrying, and other simple jobs to do, and after the day's work was completed, he was sent into the town to beg for food. Luther took it all as an essential part of his training, and in return, he looked to the tranquillity of the monastery and the companionship of holy men to help him attain peace of mind. He was bitterly disappointed.

The more he tried to live a holy life, the more he realised how utterly impossible it was. The more he tried to find help from the other monks, the more dejected he grew at their shallow lives and empty chatter. Nevertheless, he took everything absolutely seriously—even to the extent of inflicting

punishment and torture on himself in an effort to 'purify'
himself. Sometimes he rendered himself unconscious through
pain, but whatever he did, he could not improve himself and
he couldn't banish impure thoughts or selfish feelings and
desires.

The day came for the Erfurt monastery to be visited by
von Staupitz—doctor of divinity, founder of the University
of Wittenberg and Vicar general of all the Augustinian
monasteries in Germany. As Staupitz walked round the
cloisters, there was one young monk he could not help
noticing. It was Luther. He was unmistakable. His sunken
eyes and wasted frame betrayed his lack of sleep and his
constant fasting, while his dejected expression revealed that
he had failed to find any spiritual peace as a monk. Finding
out Luther's name, Staupitz went up to him.

"Why are you so sad, brother Martin?" he asked.

"Ah," replied Luther, "I don't know what will become of
me . . . it is useless that I make vows to God, sin is still the
strongest thing in me."

"Oh, my friend," said Staupitz, "over a thousand times I
have vowed to God to live righteously and I have never kept
my vows. Now I make no more promises for I know I cannot
keep them. If God will not show me mercy for the sake of
Christ, I shall never stand before Him. If you want to be
converted, do not be eager to learn about all this self-denial
and discipline and all these tortures—love Him who first loved
you."

This was certainly a new thought for Luther. He had
approached religion entirely to get the spiritual comfort that
he wanted. He had even punished himself mercilessly to get
peace—but he hadn't started with God. He had always thought
of God as a hard creator, a hard taskmaster and a hard judge.
Now he had a new starting point in his search for God. Trust
God as a God of love. But it was no more than a starting
point. He still thought that he had to earn his salvation by
doing all the things which the Church demanded.

Luther had spent two years as a monk in the dark cloisters
of the monastery when he was made a priest. Much of the
time he had created a diversion from his confused feelings by
devoting himself to considerable study. In a damp, dark cell

lit by a shaft of light from a small window-opening and with a candle flickering over his parchments, Luther grappled with the Greek and Hebrew texts of the Bible.

Staupitz took a close interest in him and arranged with the ruler of Saxony for Luther to become a professor of philosophy at Wittenberg University. He was taken out of the service of the monastery and moved to Wittenberg where he was given a cell in a small 'Augustinian Cloister'.

Then, in the middle of all this activity, when he was twenty-six, Luther was called to make a journey which made a tremendous difference to his whole outlook. He was selected by a group of monasteries to represent their interests in a visit to the Pope at Rome. Luther grasped at the opportunity, for he imagined that Rome was the very heart of Godliness—the centre of the Holy Church. He felt sure that he would derive new and vital experience from the visit. Eagerly he set out on the Southward journey across the Alps.

On his way, he was amazed by the wealth and hypocrisy of some of the monasteries he visited. But he was to be more surprised by Rome itself. Luther started off like a wide-eyed schoolboy, drinking in all the superstition and ceremonial, believing all that he was told and eagerly taking part in all the services and ritual. But he discovered that the priests of Rome laughed at his seriousness and sincerity. He found that they rattled through their prayers and services with an indifference which made him feel sick. The more he spoke to priests, bishops and other dignitaries, whether in private or over the dinner table, the more he found hypocrisy and irreverence for the things of God.

Above all, he found that the city which was the centre of the 'Holy Church' had the worst crime rate of any place he had set foot in, despite its great number of priests and churches. "No one can imagine the sins and scandalous crimes committed in Rome," he said. "The city is filled with chaos and murder." Luther had never for one moment suspected the things which he saw, but Rome demolished in one stroke all his naivity and superstitious belief.

He had given up his life to the Roman Catholic Church because the Church claimed the power to forgive sins and save souls. He had found that nothing which the Church did

Martin Luther, second from left with his fellow reform

really worked. Although he had become a monk, passed the theological examinations and been made a priest, he had no consciousness that his sins were forgiven and no awareness that he was in touch with God. None of the penances, fastings, services or chanting had helped one bit. His only remaining hope had been to pin everything on the power of the Holy Church in blind trust. He thought that if the Holy Church said this was the way to God—it MUST be right.

The fatal visit to Rome shattered his last vestige of trust. He found that the 'Holy Church' had no magic or holiness at all, and that a vast proportion of it was not even sincere. He lost all confidence in the pomp and ceremony. It is not surprising that when Luther returned to Wittenberg, he was more anxious than ever to understand what the Bible had to say about true religion and the way to find God.

Dr. Staupitz detected Luther's desire and pressed him to study for the degree of doctor of theology so that he could devote himself to studying and teaching the Bible. Luther set himself to the task and achieved the degree two years later, aged twenty-eight. Then he began giving regular afternoon lectures to students, as Wittenberg's Professor of the Bible.

For ten years, he had followed what the Church of Rome said about salvation. Now he searched the Bible for answers. He saw that only self-righteous scribes and pharisees thought themselves able to earn God's favour—and they were rejected by the Lord Jesus Christ. He saw that, according to the Scriptures, "all have sinned and come short of the glory of God."

Then Luther read of how the Lord Jesus Christ had come to die on the cross of Calvary to bear the punishment of man's sin, so that all who genuinely repented could be freely forgiven. He grew to understand the process by which God receives a man. It was not by commanding him into a monastery to perform meaningless tasks and ritual, at the same time denying him any real contact with Himself. Luther saw in the Bible that God gives a man who comes to Him a definite, unmistakable experience, so that he feels and knows that his sins are forgiven and that God has accepted him.

He saw that God 'converts' a man, gives him a 'new birth', a new heart, a new outlook and opens his eyes to an understanding of the Bible.

Luther was thirty years of age when he had this very experience himself. He was sitting in his cell studying the New Testament (Paul's letter to the Romans) when he came across these words: "The just shall live by faith" (Romans 1:17).

"My situation was that, although an impeccable monk, I stood before God as a sinner troubled in conscience and had no confidence that my character would satisfy Him.

"Night and day I pondered until I saw the meaning of 'the just shall live by faith'. Then I grasped that the justice of God is the righteousness by which, through grace and sheer mercy, He justifies us through faith. Immediately I felt myself to have been reborn and to have gone through open doors into paradise."

Martin Luther's momentous experience opened his eyes to understand the ways of God and the truth of the Bible. Soon after his experience, he became increasingly appalled at the commercialisation and hypocrisy of the Roman Catholic Church. His dissatisfaction was brought to a head when monks went to Wittenberg from Rome, raising money for the building of St. Peter's, Rome, by 'selling' the Pope's pardon for sins (indulgences). On the eve of a great religious festival, when great crowds gathered in the town, Luther nailed to the church door his famous 'Ninety-five Theses' in which he denounced the sale of indulgences and denied that the Pope could forgive sins.

The struggle to break the fetters of superstitious, man-made religion had begun. By the time of his death twenty-nine years later, Luther had become the great reformer whom God used to usher in the Reformation of Europe and to restore the faith of the Bible.

COMMODORE OF THE FLEET

Captain John C. Brown

It is surprising to discover how many sea captains have been convinced, earnest Christians. Whether you think in terms of warships or passenger liners; ships' masters are not lacking among those who have declared themselves to be Bible-believing men. Captain John Brown, the well-known Commodore of the Union Castle line until 1950, was such a man. Towards the end of the War, as he was approaching the zenith of his career, he spoke these words to a meeting of over three thousand people in New York:

"I would like to give my testimony to the wonderful, saving grace, and the wonderful keeping power of the Lord Jesus Christ, whom I accepted as my Saviour thirty-five years ago. Previously I had been living a life which was bringing the grey hairs of my father in sorrow to the grave. But when I came to Christ as a trembling, guilty sinner, He freely forgave all, and I found His promise true, 'him that cometh to Me I will in no wise cast out.'

"Since then, in spite of all my failings, He has kept me. Frequently I have looked death in the face, having been sunk three times, twice by torpedoing and once by collision, as well as being bombed on several occasions. Always, however, I have found Him with me, supporting and guiding me under all conditions. He has also given me the great honour and joy of proclaiming the Gospel to thousands of troops and passengers who have sailed with me, several of whom have come to know Christ as their own personal Saviour and Lord, and are now rejoicing in the life which He alone can give."

Speaking of what the Bible came to mean to him when he became a Christian Captain Brown said, "At one time it meant nothing to me. I took it up on one occasion just to

95

find out what there could be in it that some people loved. I found nothing. I read in different parts, and then I put it down, remarking to myself that of all the dry books I had ever read, this was the driest, and I never wanted to read it again.

"Then came my conversion when, weary of sinning and longing for real peace, I opened my heart to let the Lord Jesus Christ come in. And at once He did, and from then on old things passed away, and all things became new. I next discovered that I loved reading the Bible and meditating prayerfully over it . . . I started reading the Bible right through from Genesis to Revelation, and ever since I have continued to do this."

Captain Brown was a young officer of twenty-five when he underwent this great experience and came to know Christ. From that time he rose steadily in the merchant service, joining enthusiastically in Bible study and prayer meetings held on board ship by Christians, and losing no opportunities of helping other crew members resolve their spiritual problems.

The year 1926 found him as Chief Officer of the Ripley Castle, where he was involved in an amazing story of human survival. The vessel docked in Philadelphia two hands short, and Commander Brown (as he then was) went to the British Consul for help in getting staff. Two men were duly signed on but unknown to Brown, one of them, an American calling himself Tony Madison, was an insurance agent who had embezzled his company's money and who had now deserted his wife and children and run away to avoid certain exposure.

Madison was approaching forty, slightly built, and certainly not in trim for the manual work which he had signed on for. One dark, very hot night after they had been at sea some time, Madison, bent with lumbago and feeling desperately weak, was making his way to his place of duty, when a movement of the ship threw him slithering across the deck. In a moment he had disappeared overboard. Twenty minutes passed before it was noticed he was missing and the alarm raised with Commander Brown. Somewhere, he realised, in the miles of dark water behind them a weak, fatigued man was struggling in the shark infested waters.

The Athlone Castle – commanded by Captain Brown

Brown ordered the vessel to turn and steam in the opposite direction at ten knots. Then, having stationed men to listen for cries, he prayed fervently in his heart for Madison, who only that day had promised to attend the ship's Sunday services.

Suddenly, after nearly an hour, Commander Brown heard a faint cry from the port side. Ordering the helm to be put hard over he stopped the ship and signalled for the lowering of a lifeboat, getting in himself with a powerful torch. As they circled in the water the cry of Madison was heard again, and with the torch's beam scanning the water they found him. He was pulled into the lifeboat utterly exhausted, with his leg badly bitten by a shark. During the following days, as Madison recovered, Brown was able to speak to him about Christ. Then, when the Ripley Castle arrived in Capetown, the story of the great escape drew agency reporters who flashed it to newspapers round the world. Along with thousands of others, Madison's own family in America read the story of the sham-seaman's escape, realising who it was because he had called himself by his Christian names.

Life suddenly took on a new hope for Madison. A wealthy aunt offered to pay back the money he had 'borrowed' from the insurance company, together with the cost of his fare home. But Commander Brown longed to see an even greater hope in his life. Calling together some of his fellow-Christians from the crew, he held a prayer meeting to pray that Madison might find the Lord Jesus Christ. Their prayers were answered when, shortly before Tony Madison was reunited with his wife and children in Boston, he repented of all his sins and became a Christian. He went home a saved man.

One day in 1928, Captain Brown, while serving as Chief Officer of the Windsor Castle, saw two distinguished looking people having lunch on board while the ship was in port.

"Who are these people?" he enquired.

"Sir Arthur and Lady Conan Doyle," came the reply. They had been invited to lunch by the shipping line four months before sailing in the Windsor Castle to tour Africa. Their purpose? To spread far and wide the cause of Spiritualism.

When the ship sailed the passengers were full of admiration and near hero worship for Sir Arthur, who planned to give

Spiritualist lectures during the voyage. Chief Officer Brown, meanwhile, led the Christian crew members in prayer that God would honour their witness and overcome the opposition to the Gospel which might overshadow the whole voyage. On the first Sunday evening at sea, Sir Arthur was due to lecture before a huge gathering of passengers in the largest saloon. Brown, who as Chief Officer read the lessons at official ship's services, was told by the captain that the morning service would be held on deck. "Read something special," he told his Chief Officer.

"At five o'clock this afternoon," replied Brown, "Sir Arthur Conan Doyle is going to tell the passengers that there is no such place as Hell, and so I would like to read something in the Bible where God says that there is such a place."

At 10.30 a.m. the service began. Soon it was time for the lesson. A great stillness fell on the congregation standing on the open deck as Chief Officer Brown read slowly and deliberately from Revelation chapter twenty. Afterwards it was discovered that an electrician had suspended a microphone connected to the ship's public address system near the portable pulpit, so the reading had been heard by all on board. It caused a great stir, and the subject of Hell figured prominently in everyone's conversation that day. Then, at 5 p.m., the big saloon filled for Sir Arthur, while the Chief Officer's cabin housed a fervent Christian prayer meeting.

The Word of God so emphatically read by an earnest senior officer in the morning had its effect. As the passengers poured out of Sir Arthur's meeting, disgust was written on almost every face. That same evening most of the passengers attended the ship's service where an evangelical preacher spoke on 'God is light, and in Him is no darkness at all'.

Later on in the course of the voyage, Brown was walking on one of the decks when he saw Conan Doyle sitting alone. He sat down beside him to invite him to attend a Bible study meeting, but Sir Arthur was soon eloquently giving forth about Spiritualism, so that the frustrated Chief Officer couldn't get a word in edgeways. When, at last, Conan Doyle paused for breath, Brown said quickly, "I went in for Spiritualism once."

"Indeed?" said Sir Arthur, sitting up.

"Yes," replied Brown, "and the result was that I nearly did away with myself."

"I told him," wrote Captain Brown later, "how, in the depth of my misery and despair, I had heard God's loving invitation and at last yielded to Him. How the blood of Jesus Christ, His Son, had cleansed me from all sin, and how, as the years passed, Christ had become more and more precious to me." Conan Doyle listened like a man in a trance. Then Lady Conan Doyle came up and sat beside them. Brightly, she asked what the conversation was about and without waiting for a reply, she supposed that it was Spiritualism and went on to extol its virtues very animatedly. Sir Arthur put up his hand to stop her and said, "Mr. Brown is all right—he is under the blood of Christ and is a very happy man."

More and more Brown found that God was using his witness in the ships he served as Chief Officer. Here is a typical letter written from the Guildford Castle, which was nearly sunk after a collision in dense fog:

"I held a small meeting in my cabin each evening and a small service each Sunday in the deck boys' cabin. God gave me many outward signs of blessing. Three men soundly converted and witnessing for Him. One lady, a backslider, was brought back to Him and His service. She gave up the world and of her own desire, gathered the children of the ship together, and held a children's service each Sunday afternoon, adults attending too."

By the thirties this greatly respected Chief Officer was elevated to command a number of large liners. In 1932 he was named to command a rejuvenated Arundel Castle, and in the years leading up to the war he was Captain of the Llandaff Castle, the Carnarvon Castle, the Llangibby Castle, the Windsor Castle, the Grantully Castle and the Athlone Castle. During these years he gained a tremendous reputation both for maintaining happy ships, and for his sincere Christian faith and witness. Then—the war.

"Next Sunday," he wrote home in a typical wartime letter, "I expect to sail with about 2,750 souls on board (troops). May the Lord have His unhindered way in and through me this next voyage."

Always on these hazardous wartime journeys carrying

battalions of troops (twice he was torpedoed), Brown's cabin was open for prayer meetings and for private conversations with those wishing to discuss questions of eternity. Many a serviceman came to find God through his help and counsel. At the end of the war Captain Brown was honoured with a CBE, and immediately appointed by the Union Castle Line as Captain of the latest and finest ship in their fleet—the Capetown Castle, which carried 4,500 people. The responsibility of the Captain on such a huge, floating hotel was enormous, especially as it included the psychological responsibility for the ship's 'atmosphere'.

Every morning at 8.15, Captain Brown held a Family Prayers service, which was broadcast throughout the ship. He recorded, "The numbers at Family Prayers in the morning were mostly between thirty and forty, sometimes they rose to about fifty. We had large attendances at Sunday services and children's services, and the intense interest shown (with many after-discussions) seemed to prove that the Lord was working in the ship."

The highest point of Captain Brown's career was reached in 1948 when he was made Commodore of the Union Castle Line and appointed Captain of M.R.M.V. Pretoria Castle, an appointment he held until his retirement in 1950. Throughout most of his service, he had been an active member of the Merchant Service Officers Christian Fellowship, and on his retirement, he took over the honorary responsibility of its magazine 'Living Links' from the veteran Captain Carre.

Captain Brown was a true man of God, called and saved by the Lord Jesus Christ to live by the daily study of God's Word. He was a man of prayer—the first hour of every single day being sacred for God—and a man whose witness reached the hearts of many, many people. He was one of a long line of sea-captains living in the service of the Lord.

Tyndale, in exile, translating the Scriptu[res]

BURNED AT THE STAKE

Bilney, Tyndale and Latimer

Just over 450 years ago, Martin Luther nailed to his church door the '95 Theses' which exposed the darkness and tyranny of the Roman Church and touched off the Reformation in Germany. At that time, the picturesque towns and green countryside of England was living under the rule of Henry VIII, while the nation's religion was under the iron hand of a man named Thomas Wolsey—cardinal of the Roman Catholic Church.

Wolsey was an ambitious priest who had climbed to power after being made a king's chaplain. He became an archbishop and 'arranged' for himself a cardinal's hat. Then he was given secular power as well, when Henry VIII appointed him Lord Chancellor of England. He was an arrogant and greedy ruler who only ever appeared in public dressed in brilliant, scarlet velvet, with two six-foot priests carrying silver crosses ahead of him. He controlled just about everything in Church and State. Above all, he was determined to preserve the power and the position of the Church.

If a man failed to honour and obey a priest of the Church, he was liable to suffer the same fate as John Browne of Ashford. He had been insolent enough to contradict a priest and expose his ignorance in conversation. Within a few weeks, he was brutally dragged out of his house, thrown into prison, and then burned alive as a heretic.

The teaching of Wolsey's Church amounted to nothing more than superstition, image worship, and empty ritual. It was a 'faith' which was imposed by force—on pain of burning—upon the whole nation. There seemed no prospect of any change in England, especially as brute force was on the side of the Church. But something began to happen which led to a dramatic turn of events. Supplies of a small book started to come into Britain and filter into the universities. It was the New Testament—in Greek and Latin.

Immediately, it met with a great storm of protest from the 'Holy Church'. The priests knew that this book would cause people to ask questions and to doubt their power and authority. But the book did more than that. It transformed men.

At Cambridge, there was a short, slightly built student of about twenty-four. His name was Thomas Bilney and he was a newly-made priest studying Church law. He was a serious young man who took his religion seriously, really believing that if he could live up to God's commandments, his soul would be saved. The only trouble was—he couldn't live up to those standards. The more he tried, the more his conscience showed him his faults and threw him into despair. So, he went to his fellow-priests for help. He used to confess his sins to them and they used to prescribe penance, but it did nothing to make him feel that his sins were ever cancelled by God. Soon, he began to suspect his fellow priests as "wolves who seek nothing from their flock except their milk, wool and hide . . . leaving their souls to the devil."

Bilney spent all his money paying their penances, then gave up in despair, and began to doubt whether there was a God of mercy at all. How he longed to know the truth. One morning, as he walked up to a group of friends, he heard them talking about Jesus. He was anxious to know what they were discussing, and surprised to find that some of them had got hold of copies of the new book which was causing so much trouble. Thomas Bilney secretly bought himself a copy and began to read. "And at the first reading," he wrote afterwards, "I well remember I fell by chance on this sentence of Paul—the most comforting sentence to my soul—'This is a faithful saying and worthy of all acceptance, that Christ Jesus came into the world to save sinners: of whom I am chief'."

He had always thought that the Church saves souls by an endless course of sacrifices of the mass, ritual and penances, etc. But, according to this New Testament, even the "chief of sinners" can be saved, not by the Church, but by what Christ did when He came into the world. Thomas Bilney suddenly felt as if his soul had been released from prison. "This one sentence did so uplift my heart, which had previously been wounded with guilt and almost in despair, that immediately I felt a marvellous comfort and quietness.''

Thomas Bilney was one of the first of a group of Cambridge men who came to know God through reading His Word. Although he was shy and reserved, he immediately began to speak to others about his discovery, and a number of them met every day to study the New Testament. Some were to become martyrs for the sake of Christ.

In the rest of the country, more and more educated people were starting to question religious things, as copies of Luther's books came through the ports from Germany. Cardinal Wolsey was enraged. Breathing out death-threats to anyone found in possession of heretical books, he arranged a public bonfire for them at St. Paul's.

At Cambridge, the new learning became even more infectious. A farmer's son by the name of Hugh Latimer was there at the same time as Bilney. He was a priest, had passed his M.A. and was now studying Divinity. But he was absolutely set against the 'new learning' of Bilney and others. Latimer was a devout believer in the magic and mystery of the Church, who used to get very worried at the Mass for fear that he had not mingled the wine and water well enough for it to turn into the blood of Christ. It was more than he could stand when some of the university lecturers started teaching the Scriptures straight from the Greek Testament. He put all his pent-up passion into a speech he made to the university, attacking the writings of one of the German reformers.

In the crowd of listeners stood little Thomas Bilney. As he watched Latimer, he saw a man of the Church—devoted to its pomp and ceremony. But he also saw a man who in reality knew nothing of God in his own heart. When the speech was over, Bilney went quietly up to Latimer and asked if he could have a word with him.

"Bilney heard me at that time," said Latimer, "and perceived that I was zealous without knowledge; and he came to me afterwards in my study, and requested me, for God's sake, to hear his confession. I did so—and to say the truth, by his confession, I learned more than in many years."

In the quietness of Hugh Latimer's study, Bilney told him

how he had found forgiveness of sins, and also that a man can know God personally in the simple way of the Bible.

"Master Bilney was the instrument by which God called me to knowledge . . . for I was as obstinate a papist as anyone in England."

Hugh Latimer's experience was conversion in the true, Biblical sense. "If any man be in Christ, he is a new creation; old things have passed away, behold all things are become new." He dropped his old ways and joined Bilney in spreading the faith of the Bible. He became a preacher of great power and many people came to know God through his speaking in the local churches. The monks saw the great crowds of people flocking into the churches where Latimer, Bilney, and their friends preached, and back in their monasteries, they hatched out plans to get rid of them.

The Bishop was incited to deal with them as heretics—but when he 'swooped' on a church one evening to hear Latimer's sermon and catch him speaking heresy, the young preacher changed his subject and foiled his plan. But he was a marked man. Within a year, the real trouble started. One of Bilney's group preached a Christmas Eve sermon in which he condemned the evil ways of the bishops. Two months later, he was arrested, taken to London, and threatened with burning. The iron hand of the Church was raised against the Bible-Christians. But the men of power had no weapon against something which was about to cross the sea and reach into the hearts of many, many people.

It was the famous English translation of the New Testament from the pen of William Tyndale. Tyndale was an ex-student at both Oxford and Cambridge. Some while after being made a priest, he had believed in Christ and felt the same inner experience as Bilney—whom he knew very well. Then he had gone to live in the stately manor house of Sir John Walsh in Gloucestershire, to educate his children. Whenever Tyndale had tried to bring the light of the Gospel to people, he found that the monks and other priests resisted him for all they were worth, mainly by spreading lies and rumours to discredit him.

"I perceived by bitter experience," he said, "that it was impossible to establish the people in any truth except the

Henry VIII with Cardinal Wolsey

Scriptures are plainly laid before their eyes in their mother tongue."

Let the people be deceived no longer by the Church. They must see for themselves. Only Sir John and his family believed Tyndale's message, and soon the opposition to him grew to such a pitch, that he had to pack his few belongings together and go to London.

If only, he thought to himself, he could persuade the Bishop to give him the means to translate the Scriptures. But his thoughts were naive. He found the Bishop hostile and the Church hierarchy riddled with guile and intrigue. In fact, he realised that it would be suicidal to translate the Scriptures anywhere in England. So, in 1524, a saddened Tyndale sailed

Latimer preaching

to Hamburg, never to set foot in his native land again. On arrival, he travelled through Germany and found Luther, who welcomed him and gave him a place to carry out his great work. In one year, his translation was ready for the printer, the only hindrance being that most printers were in territory where it was illegal to print Scriptures. Tyndale's first attempt to print in Cologne was discovered by the authorities and he had to escape with what he could carry and go to Worms, where the first copies were successfully printed.

Just when the Church was clamping down on the Bible Christians, 6,000 English Testaments were smuggled into England by the continental merchants. Soon, Bilney and Latimer were seized and sent to stand trial before Cardinal Wolsey. They were not condemned—in fact, Latimer was given freedom to preach all over England, but the warning shot had been fired. They were to teach strictly in accordance with the practices of Rome.

As Tyndale Testaments trickled into the country, the authorities grew more alarmed and enraged. Anyone caught with a copy in their possession faced the death of a heretic. At St. Paul's, a huge public bonfire was made from hundreds of confiscated copies. Then, the priests uncovered the secret distribution network and several young men had to flee abroad to save their lives. In London, Henry VIII issued orders to British foreign agents to track down Tyndale and have him dealt with.

The pace of events quickened even more as Bilney, who had continued preaching from the Bible, was arrested again. Through desperately cold November nights, he lay in a damp, stone cell, awaiting trial for heresy. When his trial came, it was like a brain-washing procedure. The Bishop of London, his accuser and judge, was determined to get from him the confession that he was a heretic, had been entirely wrong in his teaching, and that he would repent. Bilney stood firm. In the end, the exasperated Bishop uttered his verdict. "By the consent and counsel of my colleagues here present, I do pronounce thee, Thomas Bilney . . . to be convicted of heresy." The public—even the King—wondered whether the new faith of the Cambridge scholar would stand the test of being threatened with death.

Three nights passed before Bilney was due for sentence. All the time his friends pleaded with him to preserve his life. Weakened and sickened by the whole ordeal and demoralised by his friends, Bilney signed against his faith and confessed his 'errors'. Then, he was publicly humiliated and thrown into prison for twelve months.

A changed man emerged from prison the following year. Poor Bilney had lost his peace and communion with God. Nothing could comfort him. Like the apostle Peter, he had denied his Lord. There was only one thing he could do. One evening, after saying goodbye to his friends at Cambridge, he set off into Norfolk to preach the faith. He spoke to crowds of God's way of forgiveness and he read from Tyndale's New Testament which he carried. Within months he was arrested and burned alive as a heretic.

Hugh Latimer suffered interrogation and imprisonment just like Bilney—but the authorities had to be more careful with him because he had preached to Henry VIII and won his compliments. The persecutors were filled with dismay when Henry invited Latimer to preach more sermons at Greenwich Palace and then made him Bishop of Worcester. For four years he preached and worked ceaselessly until Henry insisted on certain Roman Catholic teaching being compulsory in the Church. Latimer opposed it, resigned, and was silenced for eight years. Then, he was shut in the Tower until the boy King Edward succeeded to the throne.

Now the turning point came for those who knew Christ and taught the Biblical way of salvation. Latimer was released and for six years preached to the King and in every part of England. At the same time, Cranmer, Ridley, and others revised the teaching and worship of the whole Church. The bishops and priests of Rome saw their power gone and their rule of darkness ended. But they had a final opportunity to destroy Bible Christianity in one last, vicious burst when Queen Mary, the hater of Protestants, came to the throne.

A warrant went out for Latimer's arrest. He was brought to the Tower with Cranmer and Ridley. He was an old man of eighty when they led him out for burning at Oxford. With Ridley, he was chained to a stake, a bag of gunpowder round his neck and faggots piled about him. As the fire was lit,

The burning of martyrs

Latimer uttered his famous words, "Be of good comfort, Brother Ridley, and play the man, we shall this day light such a candle by God's grace in England, as I trust shall never be put out."

He was right. The retaliation of the Church of Rome did not survive for long. Men could be martyred, books could be burned, the clergy could be made to conform. "But the Word of God is not bound" (2 Tim. 2:9). The power at work was the Bible which man has never been able to destroy, or change. It transformed the nation's worship from spiritual darkness to spiritual light by working in the hearts of men and women.

It wasn't Henry VIII, or the bishops, or any other human power which brought the Reformation to England. All were set against it. It was the power of the Scriptures bringing the meaning of true faith in Christ to the people. And so real was the discovery to all who found Christ—that they were prepared even to burn, rather than deny their Lord.

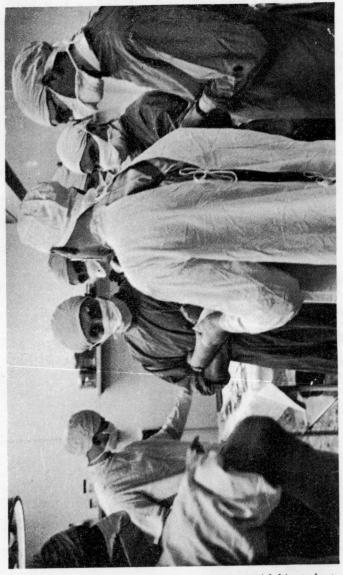

A surgeon with his students

MORE THAN A SURGEON

Professor Arthur Rendle Short

Rendle Short had remarkable parents. They had no great status or attainments in a material sense, but they were worth their weight in gold to the City of Bristol at the turn of the century. They were believing Christians who, for forty years, organised a 'ragged school' with over a hundred children, in their spare time. Also, they regularly spent whole nights on 'rescue work' —finding drunks and prostitutes on the streets of Bristol and trying to help them to find a better life. And as if that wasn't enough, they devoted themselves to house-to-house visiting for their church, Stokes Croft Chapel.

So, Rendle Short grew up to see the affect of faith on the lives of his own parents, and all whom they influenced. It is not surprising that he became a Christian, joined Stokes Croft Chapel at fourteen, and soon became an active leader in the Youth Bible Class.

As a young man, he had doubts about his faith—thrown in by the claims of scientific teaching. "I do not recollect," he said, "that chemistry or physics influenced my thinking, but zoology and physiology and geology did . . . disturbingly. Everything was to be brought to the test of the laboratory, to personal observation and experiment."

It worried him that the scientists so easily ruled God out. But as he thought about this, and read, he saw that there was more than enough evidence of the message of the Bible, to prove the reality of his walk with Christ.

As his parents could not afford to send him to university, Rendle Short had to win a scholarship, which he did when he was only sixteen, and went to University College, Bristol, to study general science. For some time, he had dreamed of giving his life in service overseas, as a medical missionary, and

E

he set his heart on entrance to the Bristol Medical School. With another scholarship won, he became a medical student in the days when surgery had only just cleared from its track the problems of pain and infection.

As he embarked upon his medical course, Rendle Short began to dream of his future career, and slowly changed his mind about going abroad as a missionary. "It sounded a lonely, squalid, poverty-stricken existence," he said. Then one day, he noticed a text printed on a calendar. "Seekest thou great things for thyself? Seek them not."

"It came to me like a blow in the face," he wrote later. And he gave up the self-centred ambition which had been forming, and resolved to aim at going to the mission field. He was such an outstanding student that one of the lecturing doctors at Bristol said, "He is the most distinguished student that we have had at the Bristol Medical School during my twenty years connection with it."

In those days, young doctors and surgeons had to get their experience by taking junior hospital posts without pay, and after qualifying, Rendle Short took such a post at the Bristol General Hospital. He made great strides, gaining the London M.D. degree with a gold medal, giving lectures, beginning to write books, and obtaining his fellowship of the Royal College of Surgeons. His unusual progress was well summed up by a Bristol surgeon who met his fiancee out walking one day. He stopped her and said, "I understand that you are the lady who is going to marry the Encyclopaedia Britannica."

When Rendle Short was married (in 1908), he and his wife made every effort to go overseas as missionaries, but all opportunities seemed to close in front of them. So they stayed in Bristol and Rendle Short decided to practice surgery there.

In those days, many operations were carried out in the homes of the patients. "One of the first private operations I was invited to perform," wrote Rendle Short, "was for varicose veins, and the lady was sent to me by one of my students. He had just qualified and was doing a locum for a few weeks for a doctor at the other end of Bristol. He stipulated that the fee must be small. We would do the operation at a nurse's house. I believe I undertook to do it for ten

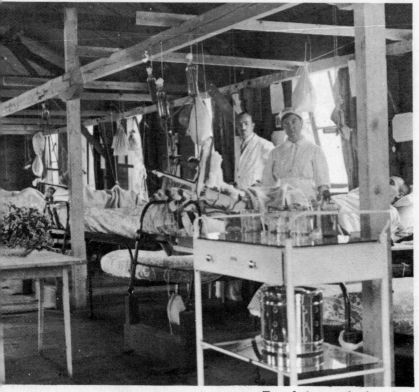

Transfusions at the front-line

guineas or so. The woman had lately come from Burma. During her convalescence, I heard that her husband poured out on her bed a handful of rubies as "a present for being a good girl"—one of them would have bought my entire fortune!"

Just before the first world war, Rendle Short was selected to give the 'Hunterian Lecture' in London, an important occasion in the medical world. His subject was 'Surgical Shock' and his lecture was printed and read by medical men everywhere.

Then the war broke out—and on the battlefields, men were dying from shock as the result of their injuries. In 1917, Rendle Short was posted to France as a surgeon with the Fifth Army. But after a few months, he was moved to undertake the study and treatment of shock in a casualty clearing

The Bristol Royal Infirmary

station, given a roving commission up and down the front line and given research laboratory facilities in a converted London bus. He found loss of blood was the main cause of shock in his wounded men and he became one of the first surgeons ever to try blood transfusions at the front line.

"A lieutenant named Edwards whose leg had been shattered and who had bled so much that he was pulseless, was our first patient. A donor was obtained and we brought the two side by side . . ."

The blood transfusion was carried out direct—one man to the other, using a piece of rubber tubing. It was successful, but a better technique had to be found. "We decided to withdraw a pint of blood into a Sodium Citrate solution to prevent coagulation, collect it in a flask and carry that to the patient's bedside. This is the method in use today."

Rendle Short had a constitution like steel, and after his return from Flanders, he took nearly all the night emergencies at the Bristol Royal Infirmary, and half the daytime operations. In addition, he frequently rushed to Hereford and other towns to operate.

Every Sunday, Rendle Short preached either in a Bristol chapel, or to a village assembly. But the Christian work closest to his heart was his Men's Bible Class, held in a Shaftesbury Crusade building in the very poor Temple Meads area. He had first taken charge of the class in 1912, and assisted by the Bristol City Missioner, had built it up to a membership of seventy men. So attached was the eminent surgeon to the men of the Bible Class, that he once said to the Missioner, "If God called me to wholetime Christian teaching and work, I would devote my life to the work here at Shaftesbury."

Seven o'clock every Thursday evening, the Class members came together to sing hymns, read the Bible and listen to Rendle Short teach. They were deeply attached to him and many came to believe in Christ and be transformed by the power of the Gospel.

He was very keen to visit the men in their homes and would often visit six or more homes in a single night. Once he went to see a man who had lived alone, unvisited for over forty years because of his foul language. His wife was found and they were reconciled. He began attending the Bible Class and was soon spotted teaching Bible stories to the children in the street.

Another night, the City Missioner said to Rendle Short, "There is a member who wants to see you. Can you spare a few minutes?" "I can," said the surgeon and they went to see a man who had been a quiet member of the Bible Class for several years. He was very ill and Rendle Short asked him what he wished to talk about. "Doctor," he said, "by the grace of God I have come to believe."

In 1933, Rendle Short was appointed Professor of Surgery at Bristol, a post which he held till after the last war. Some people thought him mean, because he spent so little money on himself, for a man of his status, and even rode a bicycle. But what they didn't realise was how lavishly he gave money to missionary work, to student Christian Union activities, to the building of places of worship, and to individual people who were in need. On several occasions he saw or heard of a large housing estate with no place of worship and promptly bought a plot of ground to give to Christian work. He also carried out surgery for missionaries and ministers, without fee.

Between the wars, little groups of Christian students were beginning to form Bible-based Christian Unions in the universities and Rendle Short gave vigorous encouragement to this. He helped with the starting of groups at Bristol, Exeter, Birmingham and Glasgow.

By 1928, all the groups had developed such ties with each other that the 'Inter Varsity Fellowship' came into being. Up to that time, Rendle Short had been the driving force and virtually the sole source of income for the movement. He was exceptionally popular among young people and students and over the years, addressed student audiences all over the country.

As an eminent surgeon, his views about science and the Christian faith were heard with great respect and among his several books were those designed to help people in difficulty about these matters. The medical world regarded Professor Short as an outstanding teacher and when he died in 1953, aged seventy-three, many medical men joined to pay tribute to his greatness in this respect.

What was the basic belief which made this man of medicine such a man of God? What was it that held captive congregations, student audiences and working-men's Bible classes alike? What did he proclaim which gave a new experience and a transformed life to so many who were influenced by him?

It was the faith of his parents—and even older. The faith of the Bible, that man is a born sinner unable to know God because of his rebellion, selfishness and pride. That the Lord Jesus Christ, the Son of God, has died in man's place to bear the punishment of his sin. And that whoever repents and turns to Christ can be born again and given a new life—walking with God.

THE MAN WHO BECAME A LEGEND

Fletcher of Madeley

John Fletcher of Madeley was generally thought of as the one man who could succeed John Wesley as leader of the innumerable bands of Methodists who fervently preached the Gospel throughout the British Isles two hundred years ago. Had he not died before Wesley, while comparatively young, he would certainly have done so. But even without the mantle of leadership, this remarkable man became a legend among the evangelicals of his day, and at his funeral at Madeley, more than two thousand local people tried to get near their pastor's grave, such was their great regard for him.

To the ordinary people, there was a certain amount of mystery about John Fletcher. He spoke with a prominent French accent, but his preaching yielded a flow of language which gripped all classes of listener. Although he worked as vicar in a very unfashionable, working class town, it was rumoured that he was the son of an earl. So he was.

Jean Guilleame de la Flechere—this was his real name—had grown up amidst the magnificent hill scenery, pine forests and expansive lakes of his father's estates in Switzerland. At seventeen, he had gone up to the University of Geneva to study for the Church, and won all the awards for his subject. It was a foregone conclusion that he would be a clergyman. He was just the type. Then, at nineteen, he threw over all the certain predictions and to the dismay of his staid parents, rebelled completely against the pious respectability that lay before him. He decided, instead, to become an army officer.

It was easier said than done. The young nobleman couldn't join the Swiss army because his parents would not give their consent, so he went to Lisbon to get a captain's commission in the army of the King of Portugal. Here too, however, his

The coach stopped at St. Albans

hopes were dashed to the ground. As he sat over breakfast in a dockside inn waiting to board a man-of-war, a clumsy waitress tipped scalding tea over his legs and he was 'invalided' out of the service before he had even started.

One hope remained. Flechere had an uncle in the Dutch army who had high rank and influence. He wrote to him, pleading for an opening as a commissioned officer, and almost immediately, a reply came. Flechere was summoned to enlist at Flanders as soon as possible. But just as the hopeful recruit arrived, peace was signed, and the bulk of the Dutch army ordered to disband. There was nothing left for a disillusioned young aristocrat to do but to try England. So, at twenty-one, Jean de la Flechere came to England to find excitement.

Somehow or other, he found himself at Mr. Burchell's boarding school at South Mimms, Hertfordshire, where he worked in exchange for English lessons. Then, after eighteen months, his father's influence intervened and the French Ambassador in England was urged to find him a better position. In no time at all, it was arranged. John Fletcher (who had adopted the English form of his name) became the home-tutor of the two sons of Thomas Hill, wealthy M.P. for Shropshire. The new job took him to live with the family at Tern Hall, a stately mansion just outside Shrewsbury (now used as a college of further education). Whenever Parliament was sitting, he accompanied the family to London and stayed with them in their 'town-house'.

After only a few months at Tern Hall, Fletcher found himself climbing into a carriage to make his first London trip with the Hills. Towards the end of the journey, they rattled into St. Alban's—main stopping point for a meal and a rest. Fletcher was more interested in surveying the town and went off by himself for a walk. As he walked, he fell in beside an old woman whose conversation took him completely by surprise. She spoke to him about her faith, and about Christ, whom she professed to know and serve. Fletcher had never heard anyone speaking as openly and intimately as this before—and to a total stranger. He spoke to her for so long, that when he got back to the inn where the Hill family were resting, he found that they had gone on to London, leaving a horse for him to follow on. When he caught up with them and told them what had happened, Mrs. Hill said, "I shall not wonder if our tutor does not turn Methodist!"

"Methodist Madam?" asked Fletcher. "What is that?"

"The Methodists," replied Mrs. Hill with a tinge of disdain, "are a people that do nothing but pray: they are praying all day and all night, too!"

"Are they now?" thought Fletcher, his astonishment and curiosity both aroused, "then, by the help of God, I will find them out, if they are above ground."

Despite his 'rebellion' against the idea of entering the Church in Switzerland, John Fletcher was a firm believer in God. He was ambitious, and his life revolved round himself, but he still aimed to be 'virtuous' in God's sight and he reckoned that this was possible and attainable. He believed in the dignity and capability of human nature. He put his aims into practice by attending church regularly, but his experience with the old woman at St. Alban's caused him a great deal of trouble. When he went to church, he had no consciousness of God's presence. He just couldn't understand or believe in what he had heard about 'knowing the Lord Christ', and the thought that his religion was the meaningless, cold and dead religion of a Pharisee would not leave him.

One evening, when the family were in London, Fletcher was reminded about his intention to look up the Methodists when someone, possibly a servant in the household, invited him to a meeting. Fletcher went once, then he went again and again. All he heard and saw intensified his concern on account of the old woman of St. Alban's. The people in the meetings were either alive with a sense of knowing God—or they were seeking nothing less than that. They placed no value whatsoever on simply being present at church. They spoke about repentance for sin; the need of a drastic change in a person which only God could bring about, called 'the new birth'; and they spoke of 'peace with God'. Fletcher saw only too well that his present faith was utterly useless and brought him nowhere. Now he began to do all he could by trying to 'remould' his way of life in an effort to discover God as these Methodists experienced Him.

So, for several weeks he watched his tongue, thought about his actions, and tried to inject good behaviour into his conduct. But the more he consciously tried to improve himself, the more he saw his hopelessness. And besides, it didn't help him in the slightest to get a sense of God's presence. As he chased down the blind spiritual alley of trying to earn his conversion, a sermon by a man named Green stopped him in his tracks, and began to open his eyes to the fact that

Fletcher of Madeley

a hopeless sinner can never deserve anything from God.

"Is it possible," he thought, "that I, who was given the Divinity awards by the University of Geneva, can know so little about these things, that I find myself learning from a relatively ignorant preacher?" But he knew it was so, and from this moment, Fletcher started to seek the Lord from the standpoint of an undeserving sinner, trusting only in the fact that Christ had suffered for his sins on the cross of Calvary.

"On the 12th January," he recorded, "I received the communion, although my heart was as hard as flint. The following day, I felt the tyranny of sin more than ever . . . I felt the burden of my corruptions heavier than ever. I called upon the Lord in prayer, but with such despondency that I felt it was a wasted effort. Many a time I took up the Bible to seek comfort, but I was not able to read it and shut it again.

"The thoughts which flooded my mind were that I had wandered from God and trampled underfoot the frequent feelings about it that God had put into my heart. Instead of going straight to Christ, I had wasted my time fighting against sin with the dim light of reason. If I am not washed and renewed before I die and go before God . . . I am lost to all eternity."

Fletcher was now in the throes of a great spiritual struggle. While tempted to despair and delay on the one hand, his great need and desire for spiritual peace drew him on.

"I was now beaten out of my strongholds. I felt my helplessness and lay at the feet of Christ. I cried out, unfeelingly but I believe sincerely, 'Save me Lord . . . give me justifying faith in Thy blood, cleanse me from my sins, for the devil will surely reign over me until you come into my heart . . . save a lost creature'. On Sunday, I heard a sermon on the text 'Being justified by faith, we have peace with God through our Lord Jesus Christ.' My heart was not in the least moved. I was only more convinced that I was an unbeliever, not justified by faith and that until I was, I should never have peace with God.

"I could not sing the closing hymn and sat brooding while others rejoiced in their Saviour. I often wished to find someone who had experienced my particular state. I went to a

The colliery in Fletcher's parish.

friend and told him about it. He tried to give sympathy and help, but it was no use. There is no peace to a sinner unless it comes from above. When we parted he gave some better advice. 'God is merciful,' he said, 'He loves you and if He denies you anything, it is for your good. You deserve nothing at His hands. Wait, then, patiently for Him and NEVER give up your hope.' That night I dreamed I had committed grievous and abominable sins. I awoke amazed and confused, got out of bed detesting my corrupt senses and imagination, and went on my knees. I prayed with more faith and with my mind wandering less than ever before."

The following day John Fletcher realised that his prayers were being answered and that a work of transformation and renewal was going on within him:

"It was not long before I was tempted by a besetting sin. But I found myself a new person. My soul was not even ruffled. I did not really notice this at first, but having withstood two or three temptations, and feeling a great peace in my soul, I began to realise that it was the Lord's doing. I read in the evening the biographical experiences of some Christians and I found that my case was the same as theirs, so my hope increased. All the while I continued praying for an increase in faith, for I was somewhat afraid that it was all an illusion. I then opened my Bible at these words, 'Cast thy burden upon the Lord, and He shall sustain thee,' (Psalm 55:22); and then I read these words, 'The Lord—He it is that doth go before thee; He will be with thee, He will not fail thee neither forsake thee: fear not, neither be dismayed'," (Deuteronomy 31:8).

John Fletcher knew for certainty now, that God had taken him out of darkness, and made him a true, 'born again', converted Christian believer. And for him it was the beginning of a new life.

HERO OF MALTA

Lieut.-General Sir William Dobbie

"That extraordinary man General Dobbie," was how Churchill described him in Parliament, and in a broadcast to the nation, he spoke of him as, "General Dobbie, for nearly two years the heroic defender of Malta." The historic siege and defence of Malta against tremendous odds during the last war, brought General Sir William Dobbie to well deserved fame.

Dobbie was the son of a high official in the Indian Civil Service and was born in Madras in 1879. As a boy, he was sent to England for his education and went to Charterhouse School. His parents were sincere Christian believers who had brought him up to know the Bible. "But the fact remains," General Dobbie said, "that in spite of their teaching and in spite of the fact that I knew God's plan of salvation in my head, it was not until I was fourteen years old that I entered into the spiritual experience which revolutionised my life. At fourteen, I came into a vital and saving contact with the Son of God."

Another boy had recently been converted and he wanted Dobbie—his friend—to enter into the same experience. He took pains to explain to him his new found belief.

Looking back on this period, Dobbie wrote, "At that time God caused me to feel the weight of the burden of my sins. It was a heavy burden, a crushing burden, and one which made me feel miserable. I do not suppose that in the eyes of the world I was a particularly conspicuous sinner. I was, I imagine, much the same as most boys of my age, but I did realise that things were not right between God and me and that I was quite unfit to stand in His sight. I am more grateful than I can say, that He put this burden on me. If He had not done so, I

127

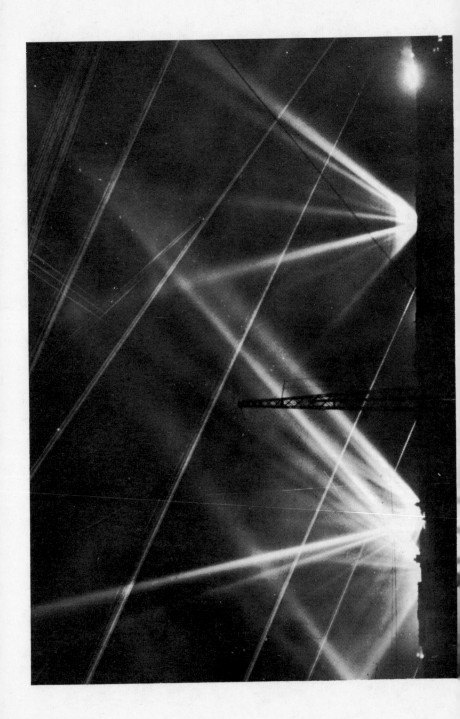

might never have sought for the relief which I found and have found since increasingly in Christ.

"Through the operation of the Holy Spirit, my need of a Saviour was brought home to me. On the first Sunday of November 1893, when I was spending a half-term holiday at Blackheath, I realised for the first time (although I had often heard it before) that Jesus Christ, the Son of God, had come to earth for the express purpose of laying down His life as the atonement for my sin, in order to deliver me from its penalty and power so that I might go free.

"I then and there accepted Jesus Christ as my Saviour, on the grounds that by His death, He had settled my debt once and for all. That was the turning point in my life. Having taken the great step, my first reaction was one of intense relief. The heavy burden was lifted for good. The past, black though it was in God's sight, was blotted out. Later, there came a feeling of gratitude to the One who had brought this about, and amazement at the price He was willing to pay in order to make this possible. So also grew my desire to show my gratitude by obeying, following, pleasing, and acknowledging Him. In other words, He became not only my Saviour but also my Lord."

When he was eighteen, Dobbie took the entrance examination of the Royal Military Academy at Woolwich and was offered a place. At the end of a two year course, he was commissioned as a 2nd lieutenant in the Royal Engineers. Being a thoughtful, thorough and methodical young man, he was trained as a staff officer, and on the outbreak of the First World War, posted to France.

Dobbie always spoke of the experiences he had of God's help in all kinds of difficulties. He was a praying man, and said, "It was like meeting an old friend in new circumstances, a friend who I had tested and proved times without number and who had never let me down." During the 1914-18 war, Dobbie was promoted twice, created C.M.G., awarded the D.S.O. and mentioned five times in despatches. After the war, he served with the Rhine Army and spent several years at Aldershot as a staff officer. Then came further promotion and appointment to an intensely interesting and responsible post at the War Office.

Speaking of this time of his life, he said, "I experienced the help of God in all sorts of circumstances. I saw His overruling control in my life and His guidance in my affairs. I have been amazed at His faithfulness to me in spite of much unfaithfulness on my part toward Him."

His experience in 1928 while a colonel at the War Office is a good example of this. He liked his job and valued it highly. A responsible post at the War Office seemed a good pathway for his future career. Then, without warning, Dobbie was posted away from everything which seemed to matter and given a less important task with an ordinary 'working' unit at Chester. He was very disappointed and perplexed, wondering why his prospects should change so quickly. But there were further unseen changes ahead. From Chester, he was soon promoted to command the Cairo Brigade in Egypt—something which would not have been possible if he had still been at the War Office.

Then he was selected to keep the 'peace of Jerusalem' in the troubles of 1929. In the summer of that year, serious disturbances broke out in Palestine between the Arabs and the Jews. Troops and warships were rushed in from Egypt and Dobbie was sent to command the combined operations of all three services. He established his H.Q. in Jerusalem and acted with great speed. As troops arrived, he despatched them to emergency areas. But before the bulk of the troops arrived, he received a message that 5,000 armed Bedouin were travelling up to attack the town of Gaza. At Gaza, there was a large population and a British Mission hospital staffed by British doctors and nurses with their families.

If the Bedouin entered Gaza, the place would be reduced to a shambles and the people murdered. All that Dobbie had available to send was a railway engine and truck carrying some machine guns. This would patrol the railway line which the Bedouin would have to cross to get to Gaza. But what a hopeless patrol! How impossible it would be to locate and stop 5,000 tribesmen. As time went by, Dobbie received reports that the Bedouin were getting nearer to Gaza. Then he turned to his Saviour in prayer. "I knelt and told Him that I was at the end of my resources and implored His help."

At the same time, Dr. Hargreaves, director of the Mission

Hospital, was also in Jerusalem. He had heard of the danger but it was impossible for him to get back to Gaza. He also was fervently praying to God. That evening, for no apparent reason, the Bedouin stopped their advance, changed direction and spent the night in open country. The following morning, H.M.S. Courageous landed a battalion of troops in Jaffa and Dobbie sent them straight to Gaza. The Bedouin delayed for so long, that the new battalion was able to take up position. Then, a political officer persuaded the Bedouin to withdraw.

"Many a time," said Dobbie, "have I sought God's help and guidance in my official life, sometimes in small matters and sometimes in big ones, both in peace and war, and I can confidently assert that the promise of James 1:5 is no idle or fanciful one. 'If any of you lacks wisdom, let him ask God . . .' It is a wonderful reality . . . providing one fulfils the conditions laid down."

Dobbie successfully located the trouble makers in Palestine and rounded them up before the violence grew into national disorder. His success in organising the whole operation was rewarded by a C.B. and when he was brought home from Cairo three years later, he was promoted Major-General. General Dobbie served for three years as Commandant of the School of Military Engineering before going out to Malaya as General Officer Commanding (now a Lieutenant-General). There he stayed until 1939 when he was 'retired off', having passed his sixtieth birthday. So, when the Second World War broke out, Dobbie was a retired general anxious to be able to serve in some way.

On April 18th 1940, he had just finished lunch when he was told that General Sir Edmund Ironside wanted to see him. It was to ask this question: "Will you go to Malta?" "Certainly," said General Dobbie, "in what capacity?" "As Governor," came the reply. This was beyond Dobbie's wildest imagination. Nevertheless, just ten days after that interview, General Dobbie and his wife landed in Malta. Neither they, nor the people at home in Britain, realised what lay only a few weeks ahead. At that time, the British Empire stood alone against Germany—France having been crushed. The Island Fortress of Malta was a lonely British base only sixty miles from Sicily (off Southern Italy) and 1,000 miles

General Dobbie and his wife landing in Malta

from Gibraltar (the nearest friendly base). So, when Italy entered the war in the summer of 1940 on the side of Germany, Malta was plunged into the front line. She became an essential British base and she had to be held at all costs.

The Italians had boasted that they could capture Malta in a day or two and they began to direct heavy bombing at the Island. The garrison defences were hopelessly inadequate. All Dobbie had at his disposal were five weak battalions, sixteen obsolete anti-aircraft guns and the guns of H.M.S. Terror in the harbour. London had nothing to send except a telegram from General Ironside. It read: "Deuteronomy chapter 3 verse 22." ('Ye shall not fear them for the Lord your God, He shall fight for you').

Clearing away the ruins of the Valetta Opera House

General Dobbie, as Governor and Commander-in-Chief, issued a Special Order of the Day urging everyone to seek God's help and protection. There were no aircraft to defend Malta until four old Gloster Gladiator fighters were found in crates in the naval dockyard. These, flown by seaplane pilots with no previous experience of fighters, were the sole aerial defence for three months.

On the ground, Dobbie organised defence measures for his crowded Island of 270,000 people. Normally, a military commander would have evacuated the women and children, but on Malta, this was impossible. Conscription, rationing, rehousing and medical relief had to be arranged. Old underground tunnels were renovated and new ones dug for air raid shelters. The dockyard forges turned out thousands of picks and miners excavated deep into the soft limestone until thirteen miles of new tunnels were completed.

During the two years of 'siege', Malta sustained 2,000 bombing raids destroying 37,000 buildings. The Times said, "It is evident that the Germans are prepared to face almost any losses in their effort to reduce Malta to impotence. In this David and Goliath struggle, many aircraft are kept in Sicily to batter the Island." Despite all this and despite the fact that Malta is the most densely populated place in the world, for every 200 people, only one life was lost.

General Dobbie found it particularly noteworthy that the Italians never invaded Malta. "It is a remarkable thing that the attempt was not made," he said, "especially in the early days of the siege when we were so weak . . . why? We are justified in asking another question. Why did not the Germans invade Great Britain immediately after Dunkirk? It seems that our two enemies each made a colossal blunder. The only reason which I can find and which seems to cover the facts is that in each case, God's restraining hand kept them from attacking us at a time when we were very ill-prepared to meet such an attack."

As Governor of Malta, General Dobbie was known by the title 'His Excellency', and housed in San Anton Palace. Part of his function was to preside over the daily proceedings of the Maltese Parliament. Home life at the Palace was unpretentious and simple. The great feature of the 'Palace routine' was Dobbie's nightly, drawing-room prayer meeting. Many influential visitors to the Island were struck by the earnestness and sincerity of these times of prayer when the Governor brought before his Saviour all those on the Island in his care.

The Island Information Officer, Major Francis Gerard, said that there was no favouritism under Dobbie;" . . . all might expect a square deal . . . there would be no fear of any 'Palace clique' running the show. In point of fact, when certain vested interests attempted to influence him, they found themselves looking into a pair of very bleak blue eyes and heard the Governor return them an uncompromising 'No'."

"In the two years I was privileged to know him," said Major Gerard, "I never knew him do an unjust and an unkind thing. His courage and example were infectious. He was a big man—in every way."

Personal courage was one of General Dobbie's special attributes. Some found it very uncomfortable to have to be with the General, especially when the bombing raids were at their worst, because he would invariably be on a roof-top watching the fate of his Island. Under his leadership, the morale of the troops and the civilian population was kept high. He frequently broadcast to his people over the Island 'public address' system and made no secret of his own faith and dependence on God.

The bombing of Malta rose to a crescendo in April 1942 and in that month, over 100 aircraft were shot down by the anti-aircraft guns of the Island. The following month, Sir William Dobbie was brought home to England.

"In the dual office of Governor and Commander-in-Chief, Sir William Dobbie has been subjected to an immense strain in leading the defence of Malta . . . his leadership of the Island fortress has won not only the confidence but the admiration of the Government." That was the official statement. And Churchill, speaking in a broadcast to the nation, said, "We welcome back to our shores General Dobbie, for nearly two years the heroic defender of Malta."

The month before Dobbie returned to England, the King had written to him, making the award of the George Cross to the whole Island of Malta. When Dobbie arrived in London, he was received in audience by the King and created G.C.M.G.

When the war was over, he addressed meetings in many parts of the world, telling of the things God had done in his own experience. To the nation, he wrote these words. "In spite of the way God has been speaking to us in judgement and in mercy, we as a nation have not turned to Him . . . He is still largely crowded out of our lives and is ignored and disregarded by us—all this in spite of what He has done for us. May God open the eyes of our nation to see and open their ears to hear, and may we humbly acknowledge our sin and turn to Him."

Of his own experience with Christ down the years, he said, "Often I have grieved and disappointed Him. And yet, through it all, I am amazed at His forbearance and kindness to me. These thoughts create . . . an intense feeling of gratitude to the One who has stood by me in spite of all. I desire to emphasize, especially to the rising generation, that it is a practical and intensely real thing to let Christ come into one's life, and today, as ever before, it is no vain thing to trust in the living God."

For God so loved the world, that He gave His only begotten Son, that whosoever believeth in Him should not perish, but have everlasting life. (John 3.16).

* * * * * * * *

I heard the voice of Jesus say,
    "Come unto Me and rest:
Lay down, thou weary one, lay down
    Thy head upon My breast."
I came to Jesus as I was,
    Weary, and worn, and sad,
I found in Him a resting-place,
    And He has made me glad.

I heard the voice of Jesus say,
    "Behold, I freely give
The living water — thirsty one
    Stoop down, and drink, and live."
I came to Jesus, and I drank
    Of that life-giving stream;
My thirst was quenched, my soul revived,
    And now I live in Him.

I heard the voice of Jesus say,
    "I am this dark world's Light.
Look unto Me; thy morn shall rise,
    And all thy day be bright."
I looked to Jesus, and I found
    In Him my Star, my Sun;
And in that life of life I'll walk,
    Till travelling days are done.

                Horatius Bonar.